Days of My Life

Days of My Life

Zohair A. Sebai
Translated By Amal Sebai
Edited By Mercy Larbi

PARTRIDGE

Print information available on the last page.

To order additional copies of this book, contact
Toll Free 800 101 2657 (Singapore)
Toll Free 1 800 81 7340 (Malaysia)
orders.singapore@partridgepublishing.com

www.partridgepublishing.com/singapore

Contents

"If the Day of Judgment erupts while you are planting a new tree, carry on and plant it."

Prophet Muhammad (peace be upon him)

"Your wealth is within yourself, your value is in your work, and your motives to reach your goals are more important than the goal itself."

Abbas Mahmud Al-Aqqad

Preface

I have called pieces of my memories "days of my life". My aim is to present some glimpses into my life. I was initially rather hesitant to start a book about my life, until I took a trip to the United States in 2000, when all my uncertainties and hesitation were laid to rest. This visit brought to life so many memories, emotions, and thoughts. I decided to write a book; hopefully, my story might bring some good into the lives of other people.

What should I say? And should I tell everything that there is to be told?

That is impossible, because we all have areas of our lives that we would rather keep to ourselves and not share with anyone else. A human being is a mystery. Therefore, I cannot claim that my writing will be characterized by objectivity. How objective can one be when talking about oneself?

Another question persisted: why should I write my memoirs?

This question has two answers: one answer is simple; the other deeper, complex, and ambiguous. I can easily state that the reason for writing my story is to shed some light on my experiences in life: the sweet with the bitter may serve as valuable lessons for the youth. What is more difficult is to admit that writing my story is actually a personal journey to self-discovery.

This story can be split into different stages: growing up in Makkah, my education and travels in Egypt, Germany, and America, and finally my struggle up the career ladder.

My thanks and deepest appreciation go to my friends and colleagues, Dr. Rashed bin Rajeh Al-Shareef and Dr. Saleh Al-Malik, for their helpful feedback on the first draft of 'Days of My Life'. My deep appreciation also goes to Mrs. Amal Sebai and Mrs. Mercy Larbi for translating the book into English.

Chapter 1

Growing up in Makkah Al-Mukarramah

"Shaikh Ahmad Sebai, was blessed with the birth of a son whom he named Zohair. May the child be a source of happiness for his parents and may Allah grant him a long life. It is worth noting that Shaikh Ahmad Sebai is a proponent of reviving the traditional Arabic names, as he has named his eldest son Usama. This idea should be more widespread in our Arab countries."

This announcement was printed in the newspaper "Voice of Hijaz" on Wednesday, the 24th of Muharram, year 1358 Hijri, corresponding to March 15th, 1939. Back then, my father, Ahmad Sebai was the editor-in-chief of the newspaper, which was based in Makkah.

My entry into this world came at the beginning of World War II. As I journeyed on as a toddler through early childhood, I overheard snippets of words about war, but I could make no sense of these words. Some words spoke of mysterious places and ideas that I could not understand. I remember hearing the word "sea". "What is it? I wondered. "Was the sea that water tank in our neighborhood that people drew water from for use in their homes?

And then, at the age of 5, I saw the sea for the first time in my life. This vast expanse of water broadened my thinking and enlarged my horizon.

Memories of those early years before school are hazy; exact events and places are difficult to pin down. I was the youngest of my siblings; two girls and a boy (my brother Usama). My siblings and I have the same father. My father had married three women before my mother and they had one child each. My mother was the fourth and the last of his wives. May Allah have mercy on their souls.

1

I have a very dim recollection of what my father looked like. Recollection of his face is hazy and seems absent from my childhood because he was so occupied with his many responsibilities: the running of the newspaper, an inspector in the Ministry of Finance, a guide for pilgrims, and frequent travels to Egypt. The faces that are indelibly printed in my memory are those of my mother, brother, sisters, aunts, and the other older women in the family.

What is etched in my memory is a mixture of what I can actually remember happening, and the stories I was told about my childhood. What I clearly remember is my mother's over-protectiveness and love for me, and my father's firmness.

Two anecdotes illustrate the two poles of affection and conduct towards me; my mother's tenderness and overindulgence and my father's strict approach. We lived in the Shamiya neighborhood, in one of the oldest Makkah houses; it was five stories high. I can see myself as a three –year- old climbing the stairs from the bottom to the top of the house, calling out my mother's name. My mother, worried was scurrying behind me and I pretending to cry so she would pick me up.

My father's approach to parenting was strict, not harsh, but firm. Every night he had a group of friends over in his parlor downstairs. He sent me to fetch something upstairs for him. I was very young, and would carefully make my way up the stairs in the dark to bring my father what he wanted. My mother would come close behind me, invoking the name of Allah, asking Him to protect me. Looking back, I truly hope that my father's firmness had a stronger influence on the shaping of my personality than my mother's overindulgence.

I was a frail and weak little boy of slight built. My mother constantly fretted over me; she was scared of any harm coming to me from an evil eye and even from the draft of a cold wind. If she had her way she would never have let me out of the house or out her sight. She wrapped a thick scarf around my head and neck, placed pieces of paper with writings on them between my clothes to protect me supposedly from the evil eye and from the jinn. However, by nature, I detested anything that confined or constrained me. As soon as I had the chance, I got rid of the scarf and the pieces of paper, in an act of childhood rebellion. The more protective she was, the more daring and active I was at play, often returning home with bruises and scrapes, and putting on a brave face that I felt no pain because I was a man!

I contracted the measles in my childhood and suffered from severe complications. I ran such a high fever that a slice of bread on my body would have got hot – that is what I was told! My mother cared for me as best she could, using traditional medicinal practices and whatever treatments her neighbor advised. She wrapped my body in cloths soaked in water and vinegar, she fed me herbal remedies, read me verses from the Holy Qur'an, but all of her attempts were to no avail, and my condition worsened. My father was on one of his trips and returned to find me on the point of death. He rushed me to his friend, Dr. Husni Al-Tahir, who treated me with his medicine and I was cured, by the power of Allah.

In those days, the only place where one could get medical treatment was at Ajyad Hospital or the Egyptian Hospice, or at a handful of clinics run by Egyptian and Indian doctors. There was not a single Saudi doctor, but there were traditional healers who prescribed blood cupping (bleeding) or herbal remedies.

My memories of when I started school are more distinct; this was when my older brother Osama and I attended Al-Aziziyyah Elementary School. The school was actually an old house, near the Grand Mosque. The classrooms were small and students sat on mats spread on the floor.

I can still remember repeating after the teacher, along with the other boys, "vertical line, horizontal line, curved line". The two- meter- long stick in the teacher's hand, which he used to point to the lines he had drawn on the board was also used to ensure discipline in the class. I drew the lines in my notebook, my hand shaking with fear. My brain was unable to find the connection between these lines and my personal needs. I wanted to play and run, but instead I did what I was told, and I repeated without any understanding, "vertical line, horizontal line, curved line."

It was a miserably long day so I decided that my education would have to stop at that level. I told my mother I had decided to leave school and she soothed and calmed me. She also reminded me that there was one mountainous obstacle impeding my decision to leave school: my father's fury! I surrendered to the reality of my situation, and I completed my education in the school.

A quarter of a century later, I had the opportunity to visit a school in the United States. To my surprise, children were bustling around in spacious classrooms engaged in interesting activities set up in every corner: art, puzzles, musical instruments, blocks, sports equipment, and electronic games. Each child was allowed to choose his favorite activity, and the teacher offered encouragement, support, and help when the child needed it. I recalled with some bitterness my own school years, years spent memorizing and reciting information. Could I be exaggerating?

Is it not worth mentioning that those schools which taught us straight and curved lines did indeed graduate men who later became great and enriched the lives of those around them?

To whom is the credit due, the educational system or the teachers?

Was their success the result of the school's work, or were there many factors: the school, the home, and the environment?

No doubt, these are questions for educators to explore extensively. Hindsight tells me that given the choice I would have chosen the large, cheerful classrooms where children learned through the nurture of their talents, intellect, and hobbies.

Nonetheless, I still think of my teachers fondly and I am grateful to them for the role they played in my education and development throughout my formative years. Abdullah Barroom was my Arabic language teacher. Hasan Maimesh, my grammar teacher, taught his lessons of grammar rules with entertaining stories, and Abdullah Mirza taught us geography. I remember Muhammad Saatei, my math teacher, and Muhammad Mirdad, my Holy Qur'an teacher. May Allah have mercy on those who have passed away and grant those still with us the best of health. May Allah reward them all for their hard work and effort. Each of these men had his own teaching style, but most were serious and strict, for they thought it was the best way to make a child learn.

The principal of the school, Mr. Alawi Shata, was a venerable man; Allah had given him both physical and mental grandeur. His mere presence commanded respect. When he entered the school yard unannounced during recess, the hundreds of boys who had been boisterously playing and shouting would immediately become still and silent as they caught sight of him; you could hear a pin drop.

I still wonder, where exactly we draw the line between harshness and flexibility, between allowing children to express themselves and the demand for respect? My mind takes me back to our house in Makkah. I still have a picture the house in my mind's eye; I can still smell the dirt roads of the neighborhood. In the middle of a small yard, rose our five story house with rooms for different purposes on each level, ending with the flat roof.

Over hundreds of years, the design and construction of the houses in Makkah have been fashioned to suit the environment and culture of Makkah society. One level of the building was reserved for the men of the household: the grandfather, sons, and grandsons. Another level was designated for the women, girls, and young children. The men had their own world and the women had their own private world. As soon as the young boys were old enough, they too joined the men's world.

My father, may Allah have mercy on his soul, had been a *mutawwif,* a leader and guide of *Hajj* (pilgrimage) delegations from Egypt and Sudan. Each year before the pilgrimage season, my father traveled to Egypt to get the pilgrims together to embark on the blessed journey to perform the pilgrimage.

The Hajj season is a time of blessings, goodness, and prosperity. For the people of the holy city, it is the time when Makkah comes to life, especially for those whose livelihoods is connected with the pilgrimage, such as the *mutawwif* and those responsible for distributing zamzam water. The Hajj is a time of excitement, joy, and spirituality. We wait longingly for the Hajj each year, as telegrams are sent to us from Jeddah: "the first 10 pilgrims from Egypt have arrived in Jeddah." Preparations to receive the pilgrims in our home begin. We wait for our guests on the hills and outskirts of Makkah, invite them to lunch or dinner, and welcome them to our home. Then we take them to the Ka'ba to perform the *tawaf* and *sa'ee.*

As the days go by, the house is filled with excitement as the guests of Allah arrive and the numbers increase. They gradually settle into a routine. The five daily prayers are performed in the Grand Mosque, and after the night's prayer, the pilgrims return from the Grand Mosque to gather in the yard. Water is sprayed on the ground to bring down the temperature, lanterns are lit, and straw chairs are set out for the guests to enjoy their evening. Among the pilgrims are scientists, orators, educators, and scholars of Islam, who engage in interesting conversations, ranging from science to education to religion to the society. I listen and try to grasp as much as I can. At that time, I wished I was the barber who always had so many stories, anecdotes, and words of wisdom to tell as he cut pilgrims' hair.

Only an ungrateful person can deny the valuable contribution that the people of Egypt have made to our society: education, literature, and the sciences, through their pilgrims, teachers, magazines, and newspapers. It is from Egyptian pilgrims that we first tasted some new fruits, vegetables, carbonated water, and fine chocolates. And in one of my father's travels to Egypt he subscribed to and got our first children's magazine which expanded our imagination with its stories, pictures, riddles, and cartoons.

How I miss those days of simplicity and spontaneity! A time when strong human ties flourished between the *mutawwif* and the guests of Allah. Recently,

I congratulated my respected friend, Iyad Madani, when he was appointed Hajj Minister, and implored him to bring us back those days when the *mutawwif* and the pilgrims were one, close family. He promised he would, as long as society returned to those days!

A rewarding social and spiritual event, the pilgrimage was enjoyable for all. My father went to great lengths to meet every whim and need of the pilgrims under his care. It must have been difficult for him as he was by nature somewhat inflexible and domineering.

I remember one year, in the early 1950s, my father's patience and tolerance was stretched to the limit. The members of this particular Hajj delegation had a very restrictive understanding of the rituals of the Hajj; there was no negotiating with them. It became increasingly taxing to logistically comply with the restrictions they had set. The disagreements increased in intensity to the point when my father announced that he was giving up his position as a *mutawwif* for good. Before making his decision public, he discussed it with my brother Usama, then 12 years old, and me. I was 10 years at the time. He wanted our approval so that we would never blame him for depriving us of the status of being *mutawwif,* with the prosperity that came with the position.

Before my father's death, I asked him what he had any regrets about abandoning his position as *mutawwif,* especially at a time when Makkah was becoming more and more vibrant and active with each Hajj season when waves of pilgrims arrived. He said he felt a bitterness which he overcame by focusing his attention and energies on writing his book, *The History of Makkah.*

Retelling these memories brings back sketches of life in Makkah and the society then, half a century ago. Our way of life was just an extension of what it had been for hundreds of years. One large house held within its walls more than one generation of closely-knit families. It was a simple life that did not yet know what electricity was.

Suddenly, the wheels of change began to turn, slowly at first, and then more rapidly. Electricity came. Modern modes of transportation now linked traditional people of Makka with people from all over the world. Construction sprang up in all regions of the Kingdom. The youth migrated from Makkah to distant regions that held promise of work and a steady income.

Before these changes, we lived as our grandfathers had lived and their fathers before them. Lanterns and gas-lamps lit our dark nights; we prepared our food over flames fueled by charcoal or gas; we fetched water to our homes each evening. To keep cool on hot summer nights, we sprinkled water on our bed sheets and wrapped ourselves in them. We boys spent some evenings on the roof tops; the men went to the suburbs of Makkah to stay up or spend the night.

Nostalgia takes me back to those days. Some may say that longing for the past is a human thing. However, for me it is more than that. Those days in Makkah truly had a special feel, taste, color, and aroma. People living in the same neighborhood knew each other, they helped, supported, and cared about their neighbors. I recall that when we moved houses from one district to another in Makkah, many days passed without us having to light a fire to cook our meals. Our neighbors arranged a schedule among themselves whereby they cooked and sent us food every day of the week. Today, people live in big cities. Months pass and people who live next door to each other neither know each other nor see each other. Everyone is busy with their own lives.

Back in those days, my father had many friends, who spent the evenings in our house discussing literature, poetry, and important social issues. Every month, the men in the neighborhood would all go on a short trip to the outskirts of Makkah to spend a day or two together. We, the little boys tagged along. Places like Hada, Bahra, Wadi Fatimah, Al-Jamoum, and Al-Kharar, all echoed with sounds of chatter and laughter late into the night. Occasionally, the voice of the Arab iconic singer, Umm Kulthoum broke into this atmosphere.

My father's group of friends were all educated, lively, and well versed in literature and poetry; we never tired of listening to them talk. When they tired of serious matters, they shifted on to the lighter note of story -telling. Among my father's friends was a story-teller, who created a great atmosphere of humor and merriment.

Shaikh Ahmad Al-Bassam was an amazing man. He had an exceptional sense of humor and talent in acting and telling stories, jokes, and riddles. His was an innate gift. None of today's actors has a talent that comes close to what he had. My brother and I recently paid him a visit and at 80 years of age he was still able to entrance us and carry us to a magical place with his stories.

Another means of entertainment in those days was the silent film, played on an old movie projector. It was like going to the cinema. On the days of Eid-al-Fitr, the children strutted in their beautiful new clothes, as proud as peacocks. With our parents, we went from house to house, visiting relatives and neighbors, spreading the greetings of Eid. Our pockets quickly filled with candy and coins, which we spent as soon as we got the chance on rides, swings, and firecrackers.

A brief phone call or text message or e-mail has taken the place of the personal visit to wish the people in our lives a happy Eid. I look at our children slouching in front of the television or computer screen which takes them to a fictional world, far from the close personal contact that we experienced in the 'olden days'.

Weddings were festive occasions that brought together friends, neighbors, and family. I see the front yard of the house filled with movement and activity. Gifts soon pile up in one corner of the yard: gifts of sheep, meat, rice and bags of flour, tea and some valuables. Another side of the compound has the cook and his assistant setting up their equipment to prepare the wedding feast. The rooms and hallways throughout the entire house are decorated with lanterns and lights. Children race around and the elders chat and prepare for an incredible evening. And what an evening it is!

Today, weddings are taken out of the home. The splendor is in hotels and wedding halls. The family members are no longer actively involved in the events of the evening. Participation and involvement in the wedding have been taken away; friends and family just meet, eat dinner, and part company. I cannot claim that it was better, but those days had a peculiar feel and fragrance that now elude us.

Oh! I should not forget the radio which slowly and timidly made its way into our house. It soon became the centerpiece of the household; the family clustered around it to listen avidly to what it had to say. Our house was probably one of the first in Makkah to own a radio. My father attentively listened to the news, hurriedly jotted down the most important news stories to print in his newspaper, Voice of Hijaz.

I grew up in a house that had an extensive library, filled with books; little wonder that I became a bookworm. My father instilled in us the love of reading and the discipline to cherish books. He built us small 'treasure' boxes in which to save the coins we received as our daily allowance, and from this we would buy books at the end of each month with the money we had accumulated.

My father was more concerned about us reading books than he was about us doing homework and school work, perhaps because he had only reached elementary level at school. He continued his own education by reading widely and constantly. He supervised our reading, explained ambiguous parts of the book and discussed it with us. He also encouraged us to write and he corrected the mistakes in our writing. He never refused us money if we wanted to buy a book.

By the end of my elementary school years, I had completed reading the series of stories called The History of Islam by Georgie Zaidan, legendary stories of Antara ibn Shaddad, The Adventures of Saif bin Dhi Yazan, and the Princess of High Resolve. These stories captivated me and transported me to magical places to which I escaped. My favorite hero was a brave warrior, Fayruz Shah, who faced fierce armies and defeated them single-handed. His sword could cut a man and his horse in half, and his beautiful lover was just as brave and courageous as he was.

In the 1960s, to my pleasant surprise, I found a copy of this legendary saga in the Arabic section of the Munich City Library in Germany. I borrowed it to read in an attempt to relive part of my childhood, but I was unable to finish it because it was too surreal.

As a boy, I also read the exciting stories of Arsine Lupine, a fictional character who was a gentleman thief who stole from the rich to give to the poor, a kind of modern day Robin Hood. How my imagination soared with Lupine's stories: his break-ins, boldness, bravery, and strength! I read stories of these strong heroes to make up for my own physical weakness and frail body.

Reading was the favorite pastime of my generation. It was our hobby and form of entertainment. Our literary club met every Thursday night after Maghreb prayer at a school in Makkah to discuss, analyze, and debate the books and literary texts we had read. Students and teachers competed in performing plays, reciting poetry, and delivering speeches and debates. In addition to the literature, we also reenacted scenes from stories like Sinbad. On every street in every neighborhood in Makkah, young boys were heard making speeches and performing amateur plays, but without proper guidance.

All year long, as soon as the school day was over, students from all schools headed out to the Grand Mosque. The majority of the boys had no electricity and fans or any cooling systems in their homes, so the Grand Mosque gave us respite from the intense heat of the day. The Grand Mosque was the ideal place to study, do homework, meet friends, and read the Qur'an.

How can I ever forget the summer months we spent in Taif. Although Taif is only 80 kilometers away from Makkah, it took us a full day and night to get there, going through difficult mountainous terrain. Preparations began with two or more families planning the trip together. They rented a large truck, which was padded and made suitable for seating passengers. It had a curtain in the middle to separate the men from the women. We set out in the afternoon, and our first stop was a small village where we bought some fresh bananas it was famous for and fill the truck up with fuel. We made two more stops on the first day, one to rest, stretch our legs, and drink tea, and the second to have dinner and sleep. Our dinner was a delicious assortment of cooked meats, rice, sauce, and salads that the women prepared to perfection before the trip.

The next morning, before the crack of dawn, we woke up to pray *fajr* prayers and continue our journey up the mountain towards Taif. If we were lucky enough to have a good truck, its engine would inch slowly forward on its own while we remained seated in the back. If the truck's engine was not powerful enough to work its way up with the heavy load of passengers, the men had to get out to lighten the load. They would walk behind the truck and push it up the slope.

Taif's a cool, refreshing breeze welcomed us after Makkah's hot and stifling summer air. Back in those days, there was no such thing as making reservations by fax or e-mail in the hotel of your choice. We simply drove around looking for a "For Rent" sign on houses. When we found one, an agreement would be reached with its owner to rent it for the summer, to cost of which never exceeded a handful of Riyals.

I see the picture of the Taif summer house in my mind's eye. It was an adobe house all on one level with small rooms and with a water fountain in the middle of an open courtyard. The blackberry tree and rose bushes in the yard released a sweet fragrance that filled the house. I asked my mother what we packed with us from Makkah for those trips, and she told me that we took a few mattresses to sleep on, and boxes of clothes, cooking utensils, food, and tea. Getting the house ready for our stay would take no more than an hour, and then we would eagerly explore our surroundings and get to know our neighbors.

At that time, Arabian lands had not turned into desert as a result of pollution and negative impact of human activity on the environment, so there was greenery and vegetation everywhere. It rained almost every day. In the afternoon, the women would stroll in the gardens and orchards, which were plentiful in Taif. The families that were well off rented a buggy with a horse to ride around. Taif, in my young eyes, was an assortment of beautiful gardens skirting the town of clay houses, with swirling clouds hovering above, and a cool breeze fanning our faces.

For the women, the evenings were for talking, playing games, and story-telling; the old women attempted to tell the future. My favorites were the tales that my grandmother used to tell us. One was about the ghoul or the good boy, Hasan. We sat in a circle around her to listen to stories that we never tired of. Social researchers should try to compare the impact of my grandmother's stories with that of television, internet, and virtual reality on the minds of children.

But the best nights were in Ramadan, when the usual routine in our lives changed. Workers went to work at night, after *isha* and *taraweeh* prayers, and returned after mid-night. Stores, markets, and shops kept their doors open until just before dawn. Boys played soccer and tag outside in fields and alleyways under the glare of streetlights until very late in the night.

In the mid 1950s, my father had a small house on top of a hill that overlooked the gardens in Al-Mathna, a suburb of Taif. I have so many fond memories of my friends and I as we went walking and exploring the neighboring gardens and fields. We went on excursions to small villages such as Shafa, Al-Hada, and Al-Wahat. Our transportation varied from donkeys to bicycles to cars. We would spend a day or half a day in these near-by villages, playing soccer, racing, and enjoying many other games. Our favorite food was rice and lentils, not because it was nutritious but because it was cheap and easy to cook.

I remember one particular trip so vividly from my adolescent years. We were a group of ten friends, aged between 16 and 18 years. We rode a station-wagon to Wadi Muhrim, and spent the night in an orchard for which we paid SR 10. The next morning, at sunrise, we rented a camel to carry our load of food and blankets, while we struggled on foot up Al-Hada Mountain. The tops of mountains were engulfed by white clouds, cold wind blew against our faces, and it rained every now and then. We stood on the summit of the mountain, and gazed enthralled at the billowing clouds and verdant valleys below. We rented a small room to sleep in, and dined on bread, figs, and locally grown fruit.

Such trips had tremendous benefits, not only because of the physical exercise they afforded, but also for the social skills we learnt and the opportunities for human interaction and bonding, that no computer, video player, or television could have given us. No doubt, our access to information was nothing like what the youth of today have, but I think our experiences and life skills were infinitely richer.

I am in no position to judge that one time is better than the other, for every age has its special qualities. No matter how nostalgic we are of the past, we can neither deny all that the present has to offer, nor turn the hands of the clock back. Change must be accepted with gratitude

After my brother, Osama and I had completed our elementary education Al-Aziziyyah School, we were transferred to the high school in the vicinity of the Grand Mosque. I graduated from this high school in the year 1956. My passion for reading was undiminished. I was always engrossed in a book though my interest had shifted from the tales of Saif bin Dhi Yazan and Arsine Lupine to more complex literature and poetry. I even won first place in a national reading and memory contest organized by the radio amongst school students and spent the SR 70 prize money on over 20 new books!

Despite enjoying the company of friends and my involvement in literary clubs, I preferred my own company. My books were my main source of pleasure and entertainment. A book that had a profound impact on me was the novel, "The Citadel" by the English writer A.J. Cronin. The novel was about a doctor who initially worked in a poor, rural area of Scotland. After conducting medical research, he became popular and took up private practice. Lured by the greed for money from wealthy clients rather than the principles he started out with, the young doctor became involved with pampered private patients and expensive surgeons. Later, however, he decided to abandon the pursuit of riches and return to his former rural medical practice.

Another novel that had a great influence on me was the story of a doctor who dedicated his entire life to fighting disease, treating patients, research, and preventive medicine. I was drawn to the stories of eminent writers like Tolstoy, Chekhov, and Khalil Gibran.

Before high school, all students were required to select their subjects according to their area of interest, to choose between two academic paths: humanities or science. I chose scientific subjects even though I liked the arts and literature more. The determining factor for this choice was my friends, most of whom had chosen the science pathway, and we had promised each other that we would all stick together.

Strange, my ambitions changed over the years like most children. At first I dreamed of becoming a barber, then I wanted to become a soccer player. When we lived around Taif, surrounded by lush gardens, I decided I wanted to work on the land. However, Allah had willed that I obtain a scholarship to study medicine abroad. I believe that we each tread the path that we are created for.

Chapter 2

Egypt

I was awarded a scholarship by the Saudi government in the summer of 1956 to study medicine in Egypt. It was my first taste of independence. It took me quite a while to get used to the fact that I could leave my house without first asking permission from my father. My feelings of homesickness were only partly assuaged by spending time with my friends, who had also come to Egypt to study.

I remember some names, Naser Al-Salloum, Ahmad Al-Shenawi, Abdul Hameed Fara'idi, Abdullah Manna', Abdul Aziz Ghandoura, Foad Qattan, Abdul Kareem Faden, Foad Daghistani, Faisal Zaidan, and finally, Fayiz Badr, may Allah have mercy on his soul.

The scholarship students arrived in Egypt that year. Some arrived together, others trickled in by themselves. We resided in dorms set up for the Saudi scholarship students. Everything around me seemed strange, new, but interesting. I was alarmed that male and female students mingled and studied in the same university; this was a totally new experience for me. It was a culture shock that took me some time to adapt to.

We were just at the dawn of a revolution. Cairo was at the peak of its intellectual, educational, cultural, and social activity. The newspapers, theater, and student body at the university all echoed the changes going on in Cairo.

Only a few months later, the 1956 war broke out. In response to the refusal of the United States and Britain to provide financial loans to construct a high dam at Aswan, the Egyptian President Gamal Abdel Nasser nationalized the Suez Canal. As a result, Israel, Britain, and France attacked Egypt in a joint operation.

We lived in electrifying days as Egypt prepared to defend itself and for war. Nights were dark. Young Egyptian men, dressed in military uniforms, poured on to the streets. The Saudi scholarship students became deeply involved in the events. We wanted to be a part of the important events; we wanted to participate in the jihad.

I remember a bright November morning when around 80 of us marched towards a military training camp in Giza. After one week of training in operating rifles and grenades, we were deemed ready to confront the enemy. We rejoiced at going to battle to defend the land of our brethren, believing that we were one united Arab nation, and Egypt at the heart of that nation.

Very little time elapsed before it was announced that the enemy forces had withdrawn as a result of international pressure from the US or Russia. The exact picture of what happened was and is still unclear.

This experience, though short-lived, taught me important lessons. It taught me how quickly fervor catches on, how passion in what we believe in makes us forget our individual needs and the greater good becomes far more important. I saw how easily the masses can be swept into a new movement, whether right or wrong. I realized the powerful role that media plays in shaping the thoughts and perceptions of people, and that people never really have a clear complete picture, seeing only parts and fragments that the politicians want them to see.

I am not hinting that our fervor and zeal at the time was wrong. I believe that it was the right thing to do. What I do mean is that the information that we had about the war, its causes, justification, process, and results was not accurate. Much was hidden from us. It is similar to the fighting and wars that have erupted here and there. People are fighting with or against one another; their perceptions and beliefs influenced by the media.

This experience taught me that people, without much thought will repeat rumors until they start to actually believe these rumors. Back in those days, I was stationed on the roof of a school, where anti-aircraft missiles had been installed. A flight of war planes flew above us and a missile was fired. I heard some students shout, "A plane came down! A plane came down!" so I shouted with them. Did I actually see the plane come down? No, but I was stirred to repeat what everyone around me was saying. For years I told the story of the plane that went down, until I read in a book about the war that not a single plane ever fell from the skies of Cairo.

The war was over. The Saudi students were allowed to leave their dorms and live elsewhere if they wanted to. My friend, Abdul Karim Faden and I rented a villa in the Zaytun district of Cairo. It was a two-story villa with a garden and a telephone. In those days, finding a telephone in Egypt was close to the miraculous. We rented the villa for 13 Egyptian pounds per month.

The monthly allowance for Saudi students on scholarship was about 32 Egyptian pounds, in addition to paid expenses for clothes, books, and medical treatment. We were blessed. Our daily expenditure was less than half a pound for food, and three Qurush for public bus tickets. We paid the cleaning lady and cook only 5 pounds a month. We were blessed indeed!; our living conditions were considered luxurious in comparison to the general population.

One of my most profound experiences took place in the first two years of my residency in Cairo. I lived in Cairo for a total of seven years. I enjoy retelling my experiences of those first two years because of the lessons that youth of today can learn from those experiences.

The first year was considered the preparatory year, which we completed in the College of Sciences before being transferred to the College of Medicine. That first year in college can be most challenging for students because it is such a big leap: studying at the university level is so different from high school work.

Looking back, I am not exactly sure why I had this overwhelming feeling that it was my duty to present a bright positive image of young, Saudi men. Perhaps, it was because Cairo at the time was teeming with students seeking knowledge and education. However, Cairo also attracted Arab tourists looking for fun and entertainment. It became a matter of dignity, so I worked hard to be at the top of my class. That was my goal.

I began my preparatory year with that mindset. I organized a rigorous schedule of study, from which I gave myself no leeway to deviate. I woke up for fajr prayers before the crack of dawn and studied until it was time to head for college. I rode my bicycle to college, and was always one of the first students to arrive in class. Lectures went on until late in the afternoon. I returned home and studied until 9 pm, ate dinner, prayed and went to sleep so I could be up again early the next morning.

How was I so organized and aware of the importance of excellent time management skills at such a young age? Every morning I sat at my desk and thoroughly planned what I would study that day. 50 minutes of chemistry, a 10- minute break, 50 minutes of Biology, a 10 - minute break, and so on.

I was satisfied with myself, with the goal I had set before me, and with earnestness and discipline I directed my life. When I look back, I still feel proud of that period of my life. How did I manage my time so well? How was I so organized and disciplined, even when there was none to supervise or counsel me? I still do not know. I was rewarded for my hard work and dedication for at the end of the year, I was awarded 10 pounds and received a continuous wave of praises and congratulations.

I often look back at an unforgettable experience that took place in my first year at the university. I was on my way to the university to take my physics lab exam, but was dumbfounded to find the university closed, its gates locked. I discovered that the lab exam had been in the morning, and I thought that it was at noon. That was the last of the lab exams! At the beginning of the following week our written exams would commence.

It was a disaster. How could I have made such a mistake? I did not know how to deal with such a problem. I was overcome by fear, worry, dread, and sadness. All I could think of was failure. The world around me appeared bleak, my world was falling apart!

Relief came in the middle of the following week when I least expected it. Right after I finished my written exam for botany, I saw the dean of the college, Dr. Abdul Haleem Montaser, right in front of me. He had an aura about him that made those with him look at him with awe and respect. Without hesitation, I followed him. He went into his office and I followed him in.

The dean turned around and said, "Yes?"

I asked, "Do you have children?"

Puzzled, he smiled and replied, "Yes, I have children, but who are you? And what is your problem?"

"My father sent me to Egypt to study, to succeed, and become a doctor. I missed my physics lab exam because I miscalculated the time of the exam. I want your permission to take the exam," I said.

The professor looked at me with a steady gaze; perhaps the urgency and passion in my voice convinced him that I was telling the truth.

"Where are you from, my son?" he asked.

"I am from Makkah," I answered.

"A pleasure and an honor, but the labs have been closed and the equipment has been removed. I have no way of helping you, but let me see what I can do," he said.

He asked his secretary to call the physics professor. While waiting, he talked with me to help me calm me. I later learned that Dr. Abdul Haleem Montaser was also a writer, linguist, and brilliant speaker.

The physics professor walked in while the dean and I were in the midst of a lively conversation. The dean said to him, "Our son here, Zohair, is from Makkah, and he missed the physics lab exam. Can you prepare a lab exam for him?"

The physics professor assumed that the dean's request was more of a directive than a request, so he immediately agreed. The equipment was set up again in the lab, I took the exam, and I passed.

Two decades later, I met Dr. Abdul Haleem Montaser in Riyadh. He had been offered the position of the advisor to the Minister of Higher Education. I reminded him of my predicament as a young student and how he had so graciously helped me. I tried to reciprocate the act of kindness he had shown me as a young man. Whoever plants the seed of kindness will reap the fruits of kindness.

I successfully completed the preparatory year. However, my success made me over-confident. I approached my first year in medical school with too much optimism. At the same time, I was eager and hungry to learn about the culture and literature of Egypt; I wanted to make up for all the interesting pursuits I had missed out on during my preparatory year. I drew up personal goals for myself that revolved around all the activities that I had yearned for but never had the time to take part in. I reckoned that since I had proven my capability to succeed, I could allow myself more freedoms, and loosen up the tight restraints of the year before. Another justification I gave myself was that I only had one major final exam at the end of the second year of medical school.

Among the activities I scheduled for myself were leisurely reading, improvement of my English language skills, and physical exercise, particularly tennis and body building. I practiced roller skating and learned how to play the accordion. I also attended the lectures and discussions organized by the great writer and poet, Abbas Mahmud Al-Aqqad. These were all beneficial and constructive activities, stemming from a thirst to experience life in all of its fullness.

The first semester came and went and I was involved in tens of activities except the one activity I was supposed to be engaged in: studying. I hadn't been studying, except for brief revisions. A quick revision here and there is never enough in medical school.

I was unhappy. I lacked the vitality, luster, and spirit that had filled every cell in my body during the preparatory year. I asked myself, "Why am I so somber when I have busied myself with so many positive activities?" I did not understand the reason behind my anxiety until later, until I realized that I had lost sight of my higher goals.

Once while walking, my head bent down, drowning in my worries and apprehension, a book on display caught my eye. Its title was 'The Goal'. I bought the book immediately, hoping to find in it a solution to my problem, only to discover that it was a novel.

I don't know exactly when and how I returned to my senses and discovered where I had gone wrong, but it was by Allah's mercy that I woke up to reality before it was too late. I resolved to dedicate my time once again to studying hard. I mustered up all my energy to make up for the lost months in which my progress had slipped. I studied diligently for the remainder of the first year in medical school, throughout the entire summer and during the second year. I was well prepared for the final exam at the end of the second year, and I did extremely well

I may have stumbled for a while, but I learned volumes from this experience. As the saying goes, "What doesn't kill you makes you stronger." I learned that happiness comes from working to fulfill a goal; a sense of accomplishment. I feared, or better still, I was terrified of being empty or idle. I started to find joy in my efforts and endeavors.

The words of the great writer Al-Aqqad, which I heard at one of his weekly meetings constantly rings in my ears, "Your wealth is within yourself, your value is in your work, and your motives to reach your goals are more important than the goals themselves."

How true! It is not enough to determine what goals you want to accomplish; the reasons for wanting to accomplish them are equally important.

I share my experiences with the youth, with the hope that they benefit from my story. They must set goals, and believe that their hard, serious, and sincere work is the source of their happiness and personal satisfaction. To take a step forward and gain rewards both in this life and the hereafter, our hard work should only be performed on the basis of seeking the pleasure of Allah.

Our Prophet (peace be upon him) emphasized the importance of hard work, for he said, "If the Day of Judgment erupts while you are planting a new tree, carry on and plant it."

I was keen on reaching into the rich cultural and educational environment in Egypt. In the course of my stay in Egypt, I collected enough books to create a small library. I spent most weekends and holidays in my library. I mention my attachment to books, not to boast, but to praise Allah and to thank my father for bringing me up in a home that had books.

Whenever I got the chance, I attended Al-Akkad's weekly gatherings on Fridays. I listened to him speak, pulling his audience in different directions, from history to philosophy to sociology and finally to comparative religion. He was like an encyclopedia. Al-Aqqad was once asked about the difference between Beethoven's seventh and ninth symphony and the reply he gave had an amazing depth of knowledge. And a young poet once presented Al-Aqqad with a poem of 30 lines. Al-Aqqad commented on and critiqued each line of the poem. Anyone who reads Al-Akkad's books is drawn to his extensive knowledge. Anyone who hears Al-Akkad's speak is drawn to his magnetic personality. Egyptians hold him in high esteem, to the extent that his loyal followers and students have put him on a pedestal. At the other extreme are his critics who have nothing but exaggerated condemnation of him. Akkad's bold logic has created for him a great deal of contention and countless foes.

I still remember a rather humorous situation when a journalist came to interview Al-Aqqad. It was quite obvious that she had come unprepared – she had read none of his works. She called him during the entire interview Ustadh (Mr.) Mahmoud, which was his father's name. Her questions were silly. She even asked him if his marriage was a love marriage or an arranged one, although he had remained single all his life.

Al-Aqqad said to his interviewer, "You have not asked me yet about my views on women?"

Excitedly she said, "Yes of course, please elaborate, Ustadh Mahmud."

He replied, "Have you ever met in your life a female chef more skilled than a male chef or a seamstress better than a tailor or a female journalist better than a male journalist? "Contrary to what many people thought of him, Al-Aqqad was easy-going, kind, and accommodating to his visitors and admirers. However, he quickly turns into a vicious lion if his pride is injured.

His powerful voice still resonates in my head when I remember his response to this question "Have you reached your peak in literature?"

"In literature," said Al-Aqqad, "there are many summits to climb. I have reached the top of one of them. Other peaks may be of equal importance, but no other peak can exceed it in importance."

Only someone as confident and assertive as Al-Aqqad is able to accept praise and appreciation of one's own self.

There is a lot of debate about Al-Akkad's true biography. Pieces of his life from his novel, Sarah, the weekly literary discussions that Al-Aqqad held every Friday, discussions that extended until after Friday prayers from which some left to pray and others stayed, have all given people impressions of his life though an incomplete picture.

In my humble opinion, I think a distinction should be made between a great writer's contributions to life and his lifestyle. If we were to scrutinize and critique the lifestyles of writers and inventors, we would end up with only a handful of people that we would have high regard or admiration for.

Regardless of his personal choices, Al-Aqqad has served the religion of Islam well through the tens of books and hundreds of articles that he wrote on Islam. Among his most important writings is his book on Muslim geniuses in history. I heard him express the wish to dedicate some time to writing a book on the study of the exegetics of the Holy Qur'an, but his life came to an end before this wish could be fulfilled.

Any discussion of Egypt, any mention of the pyramids and famous Egyptian personalities would be incomplete without a mention of Al-Akkad's name.

I heard of Al-Akkad's death on the radio in March 1964 when I was in Germany. I could not hold back my tears. I asked Allah to have mercy on the soul of this great man, a very rare man indeed.

During the time that I lived in Egypt, I was captivated by reading, attending literary discussions and seminars, and meeting prominent public figures such as Al-Aqqad, Yusuf Sebai, Mustafa Mahmud, and Salah Jahin. I regularly attended every Thursday evening seminar at the public literary club of Ibrahim Foudah, may Allah have mercy on his soul. It was like a shady oasis, a retreat for writers and poets. Unlike Al-Akkad's seminars where Al-Aqqad spoke and everyone listened, these were interactive seminars in which everyone took part. Some evenings were spent listening to poetry recitals by Mustafa Hamam which transported the audience to a magical land.

I kept the company of good friends I had met at the university. Together, we held educational events, lectures, sports competitions, and group trips. The ties we developed grew into friendships that have lasted until this day. It was a sophisticated community that I was happy to be a part of; it served as a healthy means of recreation and respite.

While in university, I played a role in calling others to Islam. Initially, what motivated me to talk about Islam was the challenge and intrigue I felt in engaging in lively dialogue with my Christian friends, about passages in the Bible. Our gatherings were loud, emotionally charged, and full of youthful energy.

I made the acquaintance of Dr. Nazmi Luka, a Christian, Egyptian writer who wrote the book *Muhammad the Prophet*, in which he defended the Prophet (peace be upon him). I bought tens of copies of his book and gave them to my friends and classmates. On a number of occasions, I accompanied my Christian friends to their church, drawn by the passion to learn and explore. Interfaith discussions would always ensue as soon as we stepped out of the church.

As a member of the college scouts team I had the opportunity to travel across Egypt. We camped on the shores of the Mediterranean Sea and the Red Sea, in the sands of the Sinai Desert, and other areas of Egypt. These trips trained and disciplined the body, mind, and emotions. We followed a strict, military code of conduct and operation and were often in a harsh environment. However, the team spirit came to the fore as we put up our tents and prepared our own food. Some of us, friends from those trips, are still in touch.

I loved studying medicine, but hated some aspects of university life. I was perturbed by the way some professors' private practice took precedence over their role as teachers; by the barrier between professors and students; and by the traditional teaching methods which were limited to lecturing. The professor spoke while students listened and frantically tried to write down every word in their notebooks.

Learning – suffice it to say- is best achieved in a positive, dynamic, and interactive environment. When everyone participates, and ideas are exchanged something is added to the learning process.

At that time, I knew little of the optimal teaching philosophies, techniques, and aids, but what I did know was that I was bored with routine lectures. My interest was aroused whenever someone started a conversation or a discussion. Perhaps my dissatisfaction with this one-way method of teaching is what ignited my search for modern and more effective techniques in teaching medicine. Years later, when I was given the responsibility of establishing the College of Medicine in Abha, I endeavored to design teaching methods that relied on independent study, research, group discussions, in addition to lectures.

As I made my way through my studies, a voice inside me was insistent that I would not practice bedside medicine, treating individual patients. Why did I make this decision? I had no clear answer to this question at the time. Perhaps, the image of a doctor imprinted on my mind was of the doctor in A.J. Cronin's novel, "The Citadel", who was engrossed in both health and societal issues of his community.

In my fourth year as a medical student, seated in the lecture hall, a professor who had just returned from England after specialization in social medicine walked in. Dr. Kamal Shawqi introduced us to public health as a specialty. He spoke of communicable diseases, their symptoms, causes, their rate of spread, environmental factors involved in the spread of disease, and the social and economic implications of disease. When the lecture was over, I knew in my heart that this was the specialty that took a holistic view of the health of a society, protected life, and drew together human health and our environment. This was the specialty that I would dedicate my life to.

Looking back at my firm decision to pursue public health, I am grateful to Allah that he led me to this career that took cognizance of my talents and interests. If a young medical student asks my opinion about this field today, my advice would be, "Listen to your mind and heart. Will you chose public health because it is a field of work that you are willing to devote your whole self to? Do you believe in taking care of the individual within a larger society? If your answer is "yes", then this field of medicine should be your choice. It will be your mission in life."

To relate all the experiences, situations, events, and emotions in my year in Egypt, would fill volumes of journals. It will suffice to say that I led a rich, fruitful, and interesting life in Egypt.

In my last year of medical school, I had an experience that profoundly affected me. I was preparing for final exams before graduation. My acceptance into any graduate program depended on my scores in this difficult exam. I do not know how exactly it happened, but I was seized by an inner turmoil of self-questioning. The insistent questions that threatened to consume me were these: What is the meaning of life? What is the value of my life? What is the purpose of life and why am I alive?

It is usual for these questions to briefly cross one's mind at some point in life, but they normally go away as quickly as they appear. However, in my case, the questions did not go away. The questions buzzed around my mind. What is the purpose of life? What is my goal in life? They seemed like simple, innocent questions, but which could be dangerous when thinking of these questions took root. For a whole week, then a second week, then a month and another month, the same question haunted me. What is the purpose of life?

I had to find a reasonable, convincing answer that left no room for ambiguity. That question propelled me into a journey of reading and a quest for answers. I asked other people my nagging question; I asked friends and colleagues. The reactions to my question were a mixture of wonder, surprise, and sometimes laughter. Does this question really require an explanation or an answer?

I now realize that the most difficult questions are those that need no explanation; the questions that are answered through intuition. Six months passed and the question still plagued my thoughts. All the books I read and the friends I asked were of no help, and my questions remained unanswered.

I remember that still in this perplexed state, I examined patients in the ward with chronic diseases. These patients were suffering from terminal illnesses; they were poor and practically illiterate, yet one could hear their laughter echoing throughout the ward. I alone carried my worries and sorrow around. I alone carried that question that weighed heavily on my shoulders.

That night, I fell into a fitful, restless sleep. I dreamt that I was carrying a donkey on my shoulders.

The next morning I came to the conclusion that the only viable option for me was to see a psychiatrist who would listen to me, diagnose my problem, analyze it, and relieve me from my misery.

I managed to overcome the hesitation in going to see a psychiatrist. I dithered for a while, but finally made it to the psychiatrist's office. I explained my questions and concerns. He listened to me for only a few minutes and handed me a prescription for sedatives. I left his office, bought the medication, but I was not satisfied with the doctor's proposed treatment. How could the solution to my problem be a pill after only a few minutes of being listened to? I did not need sedatives or anti-anxiety drugs. I needed someone who would listen to me, help to determine the underlying causes of my problem, and help me find a solution.

To this day, I tend to disapprove of my colleagues who have an overwhelming number of patients, and are quick to write a prescription, when what their patients need most is a listening ear and empathy.

I put the pills in a drawer and went out. I went to the banks of the Nile River, rented a row boat, and pushed my boat out into the middle of the calm river. It was just before sunset; in the horizon the fading sun diffused its brightness through the blue sky. The towering palm trees were reflected on the surface of the river. It was a beautiful, breathtaking scene.

Thoughts kept racing through my mind. Why did Allah create this beautiful picture? Must we make up questions for everything in this Universe that Allah created?

At that moment, I recited the verse from the Holy Qur'an, when Allah says, {And I created not the Jinn and mankind except that they should worship Me.}

I felt as if I was reading this verse for the first time. I live to worship Allah. I worship Allah by performing the rituals of worship and by doing good, righteous deeds. I returned from my short excursion on the river with a mind clear and a heart at peace. The question that had troubled me for so long was resolved. Finally, I found that the answer that had evaded me for months was now staring me in the face. It was a reasonable, convincing answer.

This confusing time taught me a lesson, and I thank Allah for this experience. That time of enormous stress actually taught me to turn to Allah whenever I faced any tribulation.

As a student, I tried to spend most of my summer vacation observing and training at the Saudi Aramco Medical Services Organization in Dhahran. The experience and skills I gained were not limited to the lab, clinic, and bedside patient care. I also developed my work ethic. At Saudi Aramco, it is unacceptable to show up even one minute late for work. This was not out of the fear of being penalized, but because being punctual and organized was the norm. When I started working at the lab, at the end of my shift I used to leave the lab rather messy with some blood samples and microscope slides lying around, because I was used to having someone come in and clean up after me. My supervisor noticed, but said not a word. He simply got some cleaning supplies and disposed of the items properly, stowed away things in their place, swiped, and cleaned up all the lab surfaces. I saw this happen and it served as a lesson that I never forgot.

Another incentive that motivated me to work at Saudi Aramco Medical Services Organization every summer was the honorarium of SR 1,000 per month. This was equal to 100 Egyptian pounds, which for a student studying in Egypt on scholarship was a great deal of money. In addition to the money, was the valuable experience and training I got there every summer, and of course the good friends I made. Among them were Abdullah Basalamah, Saleh Al-Qadhi, Sulaiman Al-Saleem, Sulaiman Al-Jabhan, Ali Qanadili, and many others.

Today, when I visit some of the senior medical staff at Aramco, forty years after my first visit, I find that its main landmarks have not changed, although the camp has expanded. I see the street where our residence halls were located, the same neighborhood, the swimming pool, entertainment center, restaurant, cafeteria, and library. I admire the founders of this medical complex who had such an amazing vision of the future and conviction to act on it.

It was while I was training at Aramco in the summer that I received the news that I had passed the final exam; that I had successfully graduated from the College of Medicine. I was overwhelmed by feelings of delight and relief. I was no longer a student. I was now a doctor. The days of tedious study were behind me, but ahead lay the days of work and the means to earn a living. Any thoughts of future challenges in store for me would have dampened my enthusiasm, constrained my ambitions and curbed my hopes and dreams, but the energy and optimism of youth allowed no such limits.

At the end of that summer, I got married to my cousin. We traveled to Egypt together to start my internship year. Two important people are worthy of mention at this point of my life story. The first is my wife, the mother of my children, and the second is her father, my maternal uncle, may Allah have mercy on him.

My wife had only had up to 4th grade education, after which she had remained at home to wait for the man she was to marry. After our wedding, she went with me wherever I travelled, to Egypt, Germany, and the United States. We had two children, a boy and a girl. When we returned to our hometown, I had obtained a PhD, and my wife's level of education was still at the 4th grade. All those years, she had supported and helped me and cared for me and the children. While we were abroad, she never had the opportunity to continue her education. When we were home again in Makkah, we felt it was time for her to go back to school, and so she set off again on the path for education. With her intelligence, determination, and perseverance that knew no bounds, she passed through the elementary school, middle and high schools, and got accepted into university. She went on to obtain a Bachelor's degree in English literature, all the while fulfilling her functions as a giving, loving wife and mother, host, and a home maker.

Her father, my mother's brother, Muhammad Ali Telmisani, was a businessman of average income. Truly, he was like a precious, rare gem. If I were to count the ten wisest men I have ever met in my life, my uncle would definitely be one of the ten. He was not the oldest of his siblings, yet everyone in his family came to him for advice and counsel. People trusted his opinion and took his advice. His most marked traits were his hard work and selflessness. When he died of an incurable disease, hundreds of people attended his funeral. Muhammad Ali Telmesani had touched and bettered the lives of so many.

My internship year was almost over and it was time for me to make the decision whether to return to my home country to work or accept a scholarship for higher education abroad. A couple of my professors persuaded me and some of my Saudi mates to pursue further studies and training in Germany. We were told that specialization for medical students took only two years in Germany and gave them a PhD which enabled them to teach at universities in Saudi Arabia! We later found out that our advisors were misinformed.

I went to Germany, along with three other students: Hasan Kamel, Abdullah Basalamah, and Saleh Al-Qadhi. We studied the German language at Goethe Institute, and joined teaching hospitals for study and training. We discovered that the Doctorate of Medicine we were seeking was granted to medical students after a short research project, and would not qualify us to teach as university professors of medicine. My three colleagues went back to Saudi Arabia after studying German for two years. I stayed behind to study at the Bernhard Nocht Institute for Tropical Medicine in Hamburg, Germany, and received a diploma. Afterwards, we all traveled abroad again to pursue our higher education. Our ambitions took us to the United Kingdom and to the United States.

Chapter 3

Germany

What I learned in Germany was not limited to medicine. I also gained valuable life experiences. I traveled to Germany for the purpose of education; and for the first time was immersed in life in Europe. Initially, I went alone. My wife joined me later on. I spent a few days in Switzerland. Although I traveled extensively in later years, the majestic Alps with their pure air, soaring mountains capped with snowy, white peaks and the endless green pastures below, made the most fascinating natural scene I have ever seen. The images of the lakes and the brightly colored flowers trailing from windowsills of the small houses will never be erased from my memory. From all that I witnessed and all that I read, Switzerland is one of the best countries in terms of development, civilization, and natural beauty.

In Germany, I stayed in Munich for a month before I moved to, Blaubeuren, the village where I would study German at Goethe Institute. Munich was an important center of culture and activity in Germany; a city pulsating with life, teeming with museums, libraries, gardens, and parks. Tourists in Germany who have not visited Munich have surely missed out on an important aspect of German culture.

I traveled by train from Munich to Blaubeuren, a small, quiet town nestling in the middle of mountains, surrounded by forests, with a narrow river running through it. The population of Blaubeuren could not have been more than 10,000. There was only one taxi cab operating in the village. It had a handful of coffee shops, one cinema, and about 10 factories.

A taxi cab drove me from the train station to the Goethe Institute. My German vocabulary could be counted on the fingers of one hand. I registered for classes at the institute and searched for my host family who would be taking care of me for the next two months. It was a little house on the outskirts of the village where Herr Oats lived with Frau Oats, his wife, and their daughter. They lived on the ground floor of their home and rented the upper floors to the institute's students. I lived there with three other students, an Iranian, an American, and a British man.

The Oats family provided us with a place to live and meals on the weekends. During the week, the students of the institute ate their meals with the teachers of the institute. We had breakfast at the institute's cafeteria, and had lunch and dinner together at one of the restaurants in town. This arrangement encouraged students to speak and practice the German language as much as possible.

On my first day at the institute, the teacher walked into class, pointed at the door and said, "Das ist eine Tür." She pointed at the window and said, "Das ist ein Fenester." Pointing at a map hanging on the wall, she said, "Das ist eine Karte."

That is how we began to learn the meanings of different words in German. As the famous Arabic saying goes, "The intelligent one can understand by signaling."

Our teacher did not speak a single word of any other language; she only spoke German in class. As for us, the students of different nationalities, we were compelled to communicate in German. At the beginning, we faltered and stumbled, but two months later we were ready to take an exam. As each day passed, we were able to get by in the market and read the daily newspaper with less and less difficulty.

We all passed the final exam, except for one student, a young Arab man, to our great surprise. This particular student spoke German fluently from the first day of class. We wondered why he was in our class, the beginner's level. It later became clear to us that he had picked up slang from his friends at the factory where he worked. It was not standard but slang, whereas the German language is very precise, with very definite rules. Germans may be lenient in other aspects of life, but there is no room for leniency or humor where their language is concerned. When it comes to their language, they are extremely serious and proud.

An incident with Frau Oats, the lady of the house I was boarding in, shed some light on the nature and mind of the German people. On the first day of my arrival at their home, I gave her a gift which I had brought from Egypt, a small jewelry box, covered in seashells, as a token of appreciation and friendship towards the family for welcoming me to their home. Occasionally, I would bring their little girl some chocolate.

One day, Frau Oats approached me and asked, "Dr. Sebai, do you have a radio?"

I answered, "Yes, I do."

"The radio consumes electricity," she said.

I immediately replied, "I am willing to pay my share of the electricity. How much is it?"

She said, "One Mark per month."

One Mark per month! That was less than two Saudi Riyals. The gift I had given her cost more than ten times that amount. At first, I resented her request. However, after calmly thinking the situation over, I could only have respect for Frau Oats. She could have easily deceived me by asking for a greater amount. I was a stranger in the country and had no clue how much my portion of electricity consumption in the house would cost. She was honest. She was thinking objectively and logically. A gift in her logic was just that: a gift, which deserved thanks in return, but it did not mean one's rights should be relinquished. Other people's rights are to be respected, duly paid without fail or hesitation.

I have so many lovely memories of that quiet village, tucked away in the side of the mountain: the friendships I made with people from the East and West. I remember when snow fell that first winter in Europe. It looked like small, soft, white cotton puffs. For many of us students, this snowfall was our first sight of snow. We ran outside like little children, gathering the snow in our hands into snowballs to throw at each other. We walked on the winding trail by the river every day, and through fields to get to the top of the mountain, where our language institute rested, overlooking the village below.

I completed my first semester in two months, followed by another two months of study. It felt as if the language finally had let me in. I had become familiar with its words, rules, and grammar. Speaking with people became easier, as did my daily task of reading the local newspaper in German.

Celebrations for Christmas and the New Year came. The German families were eager to invite the foreign students to their homes to share a meal and take part in the festivities. One of my teachers at the institute invited me to his home for the holiday. He lived in a rural area. I spent the whole day in the German countryside admiring fields that stretched into the horizon, fields covered in snow; hillsides dotted with rooftops of houses. My teacher's house was a typical German house, elegant and neat, with red tile roof.

The most important and central possession in their living room was the piano, but nothing else; no radio, no television, no telephone. To unwind after a long, hard day all they needed was an intimate family gathering, during which they listened to melodies produced by the piano played by a family member. I was astonished by this German family. They filled me with admiration because hiding inside me was a simple Bedouin man, who craved simplicity. I longed for such quiet evenings to escape from the noise and hurly burly of the city. I could only do so on rare occasions.

That night, I was deeply shaken when my teacher's daughter opened a cigarette box and passed out a cigarette to her father, mother, and guests, and then lit one for herself. This was an extreme culture shock for someone like me, coming from a family in which even a grown man of 50 years would never have the audacity to smoke in the presence of his father!

The time came to leave the small village, after a happy four months during which I reveled in nature and in people, and made much progress in the language. Before starting work and training at the hospital, I chose to study the German language for an additional two months, in a village just outside Dusseldorf.

Upon completion of my courses in the German language, I became proficient enough to pursue higher education in medicine. The only problem I faced was that in Germany, the specialty of my choice, public health, was to be learned through residency and training. I could receive a diploma not a PhD. My ambition was to obtain a Doctorate of Medicine in public health and become a university professor in this field, so my training in Germany would not suffice.

I had no choice but to make alternative plans; to travel to the United States or the United Kingdom for higher education. I was hopeful that I would be accepted for a place in one of the medical colleges of the US or the UK. However, my dream would have to be put on hold for a whole year. It was very competitive because the universities in the US and UK required at least one year's experience working in the medical profession before continuing or specializing. I had to stay for a year, or possibly more, in Germany to work and gain the required experience, while I applied to many universities.

I figured that I should train in a specialty related to public health, so I decided to study tropical and infectious diseases. Bernhard Nocht Institute for Tropical Medicine is a medical institution based in Hamburg, dedicated to research, treatment, training, and therapy of tropical and infectious diseases.

Classes were to begin in four months, so until that time I practiced bedside patient care in several hospitals. I worked and learned for two months at a hospital in Munich, and then two months at the Dusseldorf University Hospital. I was pleased to be united with my colleagues, Hasan Kamel, Abdullah Basalamah, and Saleh Al-Qadhi, who had preceded me to Germany and were also training at a hospital in Dusseldorf.

My friendship with my German roommate, Hans, whom I shared an apartment with in Munich, gave me more insight into the culture and nature of the German people. Hans was an engineering student. He lived in a two-bedroom apartment. I rented a room in his apartment because of its proximity to the hospital.

One day, I finished my work at the hospital earlier than usual, and went back to the apartment. Hans asked me if I had eaten lunch, and I said that I had not.

"Would you like to share my lunch with me?" Hans asked.

"I would love to," I replied.

Life in Germany had taught me that if I was invited for a meal and I really did wish to eat, then I had to accept the invitation as soon as the food was offered. Otherwise, if rejected, the offer would not be repeated. Time, to the German, is of the essence and it was a waste of time and energy to repeat an invitation to a meal.

My friend, Hans, prepared lunch. On the table, he had placed two plates of cooked potatoes, one for me and one for him. He put two boiled eggs on his plate, and apologetically said that he only had two eggs and was unable to give one up for me. For a moment, I was shocked and upset, but I quickly tried to think logically.

A culture or civilization cannot be divided into its individual parts; it must be viewed as a whole. Looking around me, the great economic and industrial leaps apparent in every corner in this amazing country have only been made possible by the German people by following a system of thought, customs, and standards that are different from the ones I have been accustomed to in Arabia. To Hans, it was not a matter of generosity or miserliness; it was a matter of logic and rationality. There was no room for emotions and flattery. He had only two eggs and to meet his nutritional needs, and he ate them both. Why should he give one egg up? I would like to make it clear that this was my roommate's logic not my own. I did understand his logic, but that does not mean that I would adopt it.

My story with Hans continues. As I mentioned earlier, a culture cannot be divided into its parts. Hans invited me on the weekend for lunch at his mother's house in the countryside. His mother greeted me at the door with her boyfriend. Hans' mother and father were divorced. After lunch, Hans and his brother showed me a house that the two of them had built. They had laid the foundation, built the walls, installed electric wiring and plumbing, and had painted the house. Although they had used prefabricated parts to build the house, it did not detract from the effort they had put into building the house on their own. The example of the house can be linked to the culture; a culture cannot be divided into its parts. All the pieces come together to create a remarkable whole picture.

When my wife and our little girl joined me in Germany, we lived in Hamburg for a year. I worked alongside Dr. Mohr, who gave me the opportunity to care for ill sailors arriving at the seaport at Hamburg. This gave me exposure to rare diseases as I examined, studied, and treated the diseases of patients who had come from all parts of the world; from Latin America, Africa, the Caribbean Islands, and East Asia.

At Bernhard Nocht Institute, I formed warm friendships with my colleagues and patients from among the local Germans and also with foreigners of different nationalities. There was no longer a language barrier because the six months I spent at Goethe Institute had given me a solid foundation of the German language.

My wife, daughter, and I lived an austere life, without any luxuries. My monthly salary amounted to 700 Marks, equivalent to 1,000 Saudi Riyals. It had been difficult to get by on this salary alone before my wife and daughter joined me. We all struggled to meet our small family's needs.

We rented a room in a house in the suburbs of the city. My father sent me a decent sum of money to buy a used car, a Volkswagen. Our diet was extremely healthy, honestly not out of meal-planning and smart choices, but out of necessity. We ate mainly vegetables, fruits, and breads. As for meats, we were limited to buying one chicken at the end of the week, half of which we cooked for dinner on Saturday night, and the other half for Sunday lunch. We ate our fill each night, and were blessed to have a roof over heads. Did we need more than that?

The only possessions we had were a used car, radio, cassette player, and a camera. That is all that we owned of the material treasures of this world. The room we rented was already furnished. When we saved up some money and bought a used television after days of searching newspaper advertisements for a used television for sale at a low price.

Indeed, it was a frugal and simple life, but we did not feel deprived or in want. What causes distress to a person is not really the economic hardship, but rather when he starts to compare his life to others. My wife and I did not have anyone with whom we could compare ourselves. We lived a secluded life, with only a handful of neighbors and friends, none of whom interfered with the lives of others.

Our biggest concern, and the center of our attention during our time in Germany, was to keep our eyes fixed on the greater goal. My goal was to succeed in the program and get the diploma in tropical and infectious diseases. As for my wife, she was patient and selfless, may Allah give her with the highest rewards.

When I share stories of the simple life we had as foreigners in Germany and in America with my children, with the expectation of their empathizing with us, all they say is, "Dad, you guys are different."

Indeed, we are different. We came from another planet to this Earth. Our children live in a world where their every need must be met instantly; where we parents are required to satisfy every one of their whims.

I can recall my professor at Bernhard Nocht Institute, Dr. Vogel. On a mission to an East Asian country, he discovered an unknown parasite, an intestinal parasite. He wanted to run further tests on this parasite, back at the hospital lab in Hamburg. The only safe and reliable means he thought of transporting the parasite to Germany was in its environment, the human intestines. Dr. Vogel did not hesitate. He swallowed the parasite and returned to Hamburg to conduct extensive research! This is an extreme example of the dedication and sacrifices that distinguished scientists make for a greater cause, for research in medicine.

While training in Hamburg, I applied to medical universities in the United States, for a place to study for a Master's degree and PhD in public health. I was offered places in a number of universities Among them was John Hopkins University, one of the most prestigious medical colleges in the US.

I was still unsure if I would be granted the scholarship by the Ministry of Education to study in the US, since I had already been given a scholarship to study in Germany. I wrote to my father, asking his advice on what to do. He promised to pay my tuition to study in the US if I did not get the government scholarship. Shortly afterwards, I heard that the Minister of Education himself,

Shaikh Hasan Al Al-Shaikh, may Allah have mercy upon his soul, was coming to Germany to meet and interview Saudi students in Germany. The meeting was to be held at a hotel in Dusseldorf.

I traveled to Dusseldorf. When I stepped into the meeting room at the hotel, I saw a throng of Saudi students. They had come to meet the Minister of Education in the hope that he would help them sort out the problems and difficulties they were facing. Each student had a special need. My request was to extend my scholarship grant, to allow me to study in the US to obtain a Master's degree in public health, after completing my diploma in Germany. My conversation with the Minister of Education lasted no more than a few minutes.

He asked me, "When will you complete the diploma?"

"In two months," I replied.

"Are you confident that you will pass?" he asked.

"Yes, by the will of Allah," I said.

"If you do succeed, and you receive the diploma here in Germany, we will grant you the scholarship to continue your studies in the US," he said.

It was that simple; all the students 'requests were treated in a similar fashion. That is how the Minister of Education dealt with tens of students there. The students met Al Al-Shaikh, he listened to their problems, and they left him feeling satisfied and reassured. It was no wonder that Shaikh Hasan Al Al-Shaikh had such a great reputation. He is fondly remembered long after his death..

I successfully completed the program, and after receiving my diploma, I left Germany and returned home. I had only a few weeks to spend at home before leaving again.; this time for the US.

I reflected on the two years spent in Germany; they had been fruitful. I had attained a diploma in tropical and infectious diseases, I had learned German and I had been exposed to a way of life that I had never been aware of. My years in Germany had taught me to be more serious and disciplined both in life and at work.

We spent the summer in Saudi Arabia with family and relatives, before going off to the US. You probably do not expect me to dedicate pages of this book to that summer, but I must because it has a story to tell. One incident in particular illustrates our perception of the relationship between the doctor, his patients, and society.

I had rented a small, old house on the hills of Al-Hada, which is a mountainous village just outside Taif that overlooks the Valleys of Tihama.

Near our house was a small health center, operated single-handed by a nurse. I spent the greater part of my day at the clinic, examining and treating patients.

The diseases prevalent at the time are no longer as common today. Malnutrition, infectious diseases, intestinal parasites, respiratory infections were mainly caused by negligence, ignorance, and an unhealthy lifestyle and environment. When I look around me today, I thank Allah for the huge difference between where we were in those days and where we are now.

The vast majority of my patients were children. I had to diagnose their ailments with minimal facilities; no laboratory tests or x-rays to confirm my diagnosis. With the very limited resources available, I tried my best to treat the patients who trickled in through the clinic doors every day. I took care of the patients that I could take care of, and referred those I couldn't take care of to King Faisal Hospital in Taif. At the time, I was extremely happy that I could help those people and provide some relief to their suffering.

Only after studying public health did I discover that it had actually been a false sense of satisfaction. It never occurred to me to question myself. Why were these patients afflicted with diseases that could easily have been prevented? It never occurred to me to dig deeper into the underlying causes of their complaints. Should I have inquired about my patients living conditions, diet, level of education, their environment?

I had allowed myself to assume that I had successfully treated my patients, but in reality I was uncertain that they had indeed fully recovered. If their living conditions, habits and lifestyle remained unchanged, then it was likely that their health problems would reoccur. As for the patients I had referred to the bigger hospital in Taif, there was no way of finding out if they had sought medical attention at the hospital as instructed or if they had simply stayed in their village, waiting and hoping for relief.

I did not ask myself these questions that summer. I had done what I was trained to do, to treat the patients that came to my clinic. The root causes of their illnesses and what occurred outside the walls of the health center were not my immediate concern. I did not think at all of any preventive measures, nor make a connection between the patient's disease and his level of health awareness, diet, lifestyle, and environment. Throughout medical school, I had not been taught or trained to do so.

I was not completely ignorant of the role of environmental factors in the onset of disease. As a medical student, I had studied the relationship between an individual's health conditions and his/her nutrition, socioeconomic status, and environment. We studied some aspects of disease prevention, but most of this knowledge was quickly forgotten after graduation. I speak not only of myself, but of the majority of medical students who graduated from traditional, allopathic medical colleges.

There may be some rare exceptions, but for the most part, doctors learned to treat the disease, not the whole person. We were not trained on how to prevent disease, how to empower patients to improve their own health, and that of a society at large. We may have read some chapters in our books about disease prevention, but after leaving medical school, this type of medicine played no part in our practice.

Looking back at that time of my practice in the small health center in Al-Hada, I realize that I was merely providing palliative medicine. I could have offered more, done more, if my medical education had prepared me to provide comprehensive care.

After studying public health, my perception of the role of the doctor and the entire health team changed. I fervently believe that a doctor's task is not only to treat the disease or the patient, but to provide holistic healthcare geared towards the individual as well as the entire society. What I can say for sure is that the road to improving the health of a society is long with numerous obstacles, and is also a continuous process with the capacity for success.

Chapter 4

America

In the summer of 1965, I completed my studies in Germany and received a diploma in tropical and infectious diseases. I returned with my wife and our little daughter to Saudi Arabia to spend a short vacation with family, after which we traveled to the United States, where I began a Master's degree program in public health.

I will stop briefly to clarify what public health is all about. Public health is a specialty in medicine, the aim of which is to improve health through prevention and development. It involves the study of the causes of disease, its risk factors, and its rate of occurrence. One of the main focuses of public health is preventive measures, such as the improvement of nutrition, environmental factors, and optimal maternal and child healthcare. The goal of the specialty of public health is the improvement of health by the prevention of disease before it strikes, and the alleviation and reduction of the severity of outcomes, if it occurs. It is a broad field of medicine that combines information and research in many different sciences: pathology, sociology, environmental science, behavioral science. Students of public health are expected to go beyond the walls of the hospital, into the society and the environment.

My decision to study public health sparked much debate and discussion among my family members, friends, and even my colleagues in the medical profession. What kind of a doctor works outside a clinic? What kind of a doctor has no patients, no stethoscope, no black doctor's bag? What kind of a doctor refrains from the use of medicine, injections and the surgical scalpel?

My mother, may Allah have mercy on her soul, once asked other people, "What is Zohair specializing in?"

The answer she got was that Zohair would be going around to the butcher's and the vegetable market to inspect and to make sure that the foods they sold were safe for human consumption. My mother's reaction was to pray to Allah to grant me success. She never doubted the importance of my role. She asked me to deal with people with kindness so that they would not invoke Allah's wrath upon me.

As for my wife, for years she was unable to answer people's questions on what field of medicine her husband was specializing in. That was the case until she accompanied me to Turaba, a village near Taif, when I was doing field research for my PhD dissertation. She went from house to house in the desert under the scorching August sun, as we collected information on the health of the children. Only then did my wife understand and appreciate what public health was about. I had chosen my path in life and I never regretted my decision, not even for a moment. The study of public health, had become my passion in life because of its potential for the improvement of human health.

We traveled to America in the fall of 1965. My wife, our little girl, Shaar, and my father went with me. We were like a small group of pilgrims, traveling to a strange land. Although my wife and I had lived in Germany for two years, America felt different.

New York, our first stop in America, was huge; everything there was big, overwhelming, and fast. We had to quickly adjust to the bustle in the land of Uncle Sam. There was no time to take it slowly and adjust. We left New York and headed for Baltimore, Maryland, where my university was located. I must say that I was fortunate to have been accepted at John Hopkins University, where the Master's degree program in public health, as in Harvard University, was ranked with the best in the US.

I asked my academic adviser, who helped with the registration process, if she could recommend where to look for an apartment to rent. She gave me a map of the city and pointed to a suburb that was about a ten- minute drive from the inner city. She recommended that I find a place to live in the area she pointed to and avoid the area close to the university. I did not take her advice because I had no car, so could not afford the extra expense of transportation. I decided to find a place close to the university. I walked around the immediate neighborhood of the university and I spotted a sign outside a house that read 'Room for rent'.

I knocked on the door to ask about the sign. An African American woman opened the door and demanded, "What do you want?!" When I told her that

I wanted to rent the room, she gave me a suspicious look and said, "We have nothing available here." The same thing happened again and again. I stopped at several houses asking for a room to rent, and each time, it was an African American woman at the door who either yelled at me, or told me there was none available, or slammed the door in my face.

Baffled and not knowing what to do, I walked to a coffee shop in the neighborhood. I met an apartment broker there who offered to show me a few places for rent. He took me to a few apartments, but they were all in an appalling condition. I was stunned. Was this the America that I had heard about and seen in the movies?

Confused, I went back to my academic adviser in the university, with the hope that she would be able to explain what was going on, which she did. The area was known to be strictly an African American neighborhood. Every woman who had opened the door was surprised to see someone like me at their door, so they assumed that I was looking for trouble. That was the situation of black people in America. They were forced to live in bad neighborhoods. Today, I believe, the living conditions of African Americans are apparently better.

Within days, we settled down in a small apartment in Parkside Garden, one of the suburbs of Baltimore. My father was going to stay with us for a short time and return home. My wife and I had a challenging year ahead of us. My wife's vocabulary of English consisted of ten words. Our little girl was just learning to walk, falling as she took her first tentative steps, looking around her new surroundings with curiosity and amazement, bewildered as her parents were in this new city.

From the first day, studying took all of my time; from early morning until late at night. I was always occupied. My wife had all of 10 words of English, and my father, half of that. The question we had to deal with, was how my father going to spend his days with us. What was he going to do: remain trapped in the house or go out and explore his surroundings where he probably would lose his way and not be able to find his way back? Being the man that he was, full of energy with an interest in people, my father decided to be adventurous and cautiously take his life into his hands, go outside and experience the life in our neighborhood.

On one of his strolls, my father saw a man selling vegetables from a cart he was pushing down the street. My father stopped and greeted him with the greeting of peace, Salam. The man answered my father in English, and my father said to him in Arabic, "Listen my brother, don't tire yourself. I will not understand what you will say, and you will not understand what I am saying. I am just looking for any means of human communication. I cannot hide my surprise to find someone selling vegetables from a wagon on the streets of America."

The vegetable peddler responded in something quite incomprehensible to my father. Again, my father replied and explained what he was saying in his own language. For a few minutes, they engaged in conversation, each deaf to the other's language. My father found his way back to the house before darkness fell. A few days later, my father announced that it was pointless for him to remain in a world where he did not understand the language and could not communicate with other people. He decided to return home, to our country. Before leaving, he pressed a wad of notes into my hand and said I should buy a car to take me to the university and back.

My wife's problem remained unsolved; one week after settling into our new apartment, she had no more than the ten words of English she had come with. There were no new English words. My wife complained of a painful headache, so I took her to the hospital to see the doctor. That afternoon, my supervising professor called me into his office.

He said, "I received a call from the hospital and was informed that your wife is suffering from headaches and symptoms of minor depression. Is there anything I can do to help?"

I said, "I think it is because of loneliness. There's no one to talk to because of the language barrier."

My professor gave me the address of a non-profit organization established by the wives of some of the professors, which provided services to the families of foreign students. An American woman volunteered to come to our house and teach my wife the basics of the English language. A second woman offered to help too. My wife met our elderly neighbor, Mrs. Heidi, who also started teaching her English. My wife now had three friends, who were teaching her English at no expense. In a few weeks, she was able to communicate in English and shop on her own.

The difficulty with the English language was not limited to my father and my wife. I too struggled with the language. Although in Egypt we were taught medicine in English, the language used then should more accurately be called Anglo-Arabic. The books we studied were in English, but in class the professors spoke a mixture of mostly Arabic with English medical and scientific terms interjected here and there.

An illustration of that situation is like this: the professor would say the following in Arabic, with only the underlined words in English: "If we conduct an <u>investigation</u> on the <u>hepatitis</u> patient, we will find the following."

This sort of amalgam of the two languages is what we often heard our professors use. For this reason students' command of the English language did not improve much. It was not uncommon for a third year medical student to use an English dictionary to look up meanings of simple words. We learned medical terminology, but our understanding of everyday usage of the English language was inadequate.

Therefore, I found it difficult to follow the lectures in class during my first few weeks in America. Not only was the foundation I had in English poor, but I was unable to understand the different American accents because I had never heard them before. I doubled my efforts to both study public health and the English language in order to follow the lectures and participate in group discussions in class. Half my time at home, I spent going through the English dictionary. Studying often stretched throughout the night until dawn.

My only break from my books came on weekends, which I spent with my wife and little girl. Occasionally, we were invited by a colleague or one of my professors, or sometimes went to Washington D.C. to visit friends and acquaintances who worked at the Saudi embassy.

What made it possible for me to endure the unrelenting pressure of study were my wife's loving support, my thirst to learn as much as I could about public health, and my determination to succeed.

I remember those early days of study. In a few short months, I had gained a lot of weight, around 10 kilograms. Because I was studying all the time, I had no time for sports or any physical exercise. On the weekends, I was so exhausted and drained that all I wanted to do was to sit in front of the television and eat and rest, as if to take revenge for the long hours of study throughout the week.

I was unaware of the severity of my weight gain until one day a colleague of mine told me that he had been looking for me. He asked the security guard of the college where I might be. The security guard responded by asking my colleague if he was looking for the young, overweight, Middle Eastern man. My colleague laughed as he related the story. I was unable to sleep that night.

The next morning, I resolved to fast during the day and have as little food as possible in the evening. That way, I sharply curbed my food intake. In two months, I got rid of all the excess weight and fat that I had put on.

I tell this story because it shows that life has its ups and downs. We may lose our way, but then a word or a sign or a certain situation can helps us find our way back. We can gather enough strength and resolve to ride over all obstacles, until we reach our destination, achieve our goals, with the help of Allah.

I made it through that first year at Johns Hopkins University. It was a year of very hard work and difficulties, yet also rich with the interest to learn, satisfaction and a sense of real accomplishment. By the grace of Allah, my hard work paid off. I passed the final exam at the end of the year and I received my Master's degree in public health.

I made a quick decision to apply to go on the doctoral program. This decision was made only three weeks before the deadline for the entrance exam to the doctoral program. My original plan was to return to the Kingdom after completing my Master's degree, and then to pursue a PhD later on. I would not be telling the truth if I did not admit that the main reason for wanting to return to the Kingdom was because of the extremely frugal life we had in the United States. The stipends we received from the government scholarship were meager. I believe the allowance I got was no more than the wage earned by domestic workers. I still remember that I had so little left out of my allowance towards the end of the month that all I could order for lunch at the university cafeteria was a bowl of soup and a slice of bread.

Nonetheless, I thank and praise Allah for all the blessings He has bestowed on us. My father would never have refused me financial help if I had asked him. I preferred not to ask my father for money. I wanted to be independent.

In addition to the little allowance, we hardly had any social life. There were only a few Arab families living in Baltimore, two of whom we befriended. There was an Iraqi family and an Egyptian family. Washington D.C., which had a Saudi community, was only an hour away by car. However, only on rare occasions did we make a trip there, because of the lack of time and the desire to avoid the extra expense.

Despite her difficulties, my wife, may Allah reward her, would not hear of my returning to the Kingdom until I had accomplished my mission. She insisted that we stay in America until I obtained my doctorate degree (Dr.PH).

As I proceeded into the doctoral program, several questions came up: how does one write a doctoral dissertation, and what topic does one choose? I shared my concerns and questions with my professor, Dr. Timothy Baker. He suggested that I go to the library and look up a specific doctoral dissertation, study it and come back and see him for a discussion in a week. All week, I studied the dissertation, read it thoroughly, analyzed it, and wrote down my comments. I went to my professor to discuss the study I had done on this dissertation.

Dr. Baker asked me, "Did you read the dissertation and understand it?"

"Yes," I said.

"Well, you should know that this type of doctoral dissertation is no longer acceptable at the university."

That is all he said and left me. It was up to me to find out what this dissertation lacked, why it was unacceptable. Finally, I discovered that this dissertation was descriptive, whereas only an analytical study would be acceptable to the university.

I was, initially, disappointed by my professor's comment. After all the time and effort I had put into studying the dissertation, he had simply said that it was unacceptable. However, after a great deal of thought, I realized that my professor's approach was right. I will never forget the lesson I learned that day. A good teacher's role is to help students develop the skills for learning, the ability to search for knowledge, and find answers on their own – not simply to pass on information and provide them with answers.

The focus of my research for my Master's degree thesis was schistosomiasis, an infection caused by the parasite, schistosoma. During my stay in Germany, I became interested in tropical infectious diseases. One of the previous summers, I had worked with an epidemiologist at the Saudi Aramco Medical Services Department in a field research on schistosomiasis in the Kingdom. For my PhD dissertation, my attention shifted to international health, a decision which was partly due to the influence of my professor, Dr. Timothy Baker.

One of the university requirements for the Dr. PH degree in International Health was that the student must conduct his/her research in a developing country. My professor suggested that I do my research in Afghanistan or India or Peru. If I chose any of these countries, I could receive complete funding for the research from the university, because it already had projects in those countries. However, I insisted on conducting my research in the Kingdom of Saudi Arabia.

After lengthy negotiations, the university finally approved my research plans on one condition: that the Saudi government would be fully responsible for all the research expenditure. This included travel and accommodation expenses for two professors from John Hopkins University who would visit the

Kingdom to supervise my field work: Professor Timothy Baker and a professor of anthropology. This would be in addition to all logistics, including a team of healthcare workers, transportation, accommodation, and laboratory costs.

The Dr. PH program, including the theoretical study and the field work would take three years to complete. I spent the first few months reading extensively, trying to find the topic to choose for my dissertation. After much deliberation, I arrived at three possible options: a comparative study of children's health in rural areas, the study of traditional medicine, or the study of endemic syphilis.

In the summer of 1966, I went to Saudi Arabia to investigate and to select the topic for my field work. I also had to persuade the appropriate officials in the Kingdom to accept the conditions that John Hopkins University had imposed.

I had no difficulty convincing the Minister of Education, Shaikh Hasan Al Al-Shaikh that I wanted to pursue a Dr. PH degree, since I had already been accepted into the program. There was also no difficulty in getting his approval for the funding of my field research, for hosting two university professors from the US, and for facilitating the logistics for the conduct of the research. The reasons for his endorsement of my research project were not only because he had an amiable and generous nature, but also because he had long-term vision. My research was the first to be conducted by a Saudi researcher in the Kingdom, and it was hoped that my research would be the first of much more future research by Saudi doctors and scientists.

Unfortunately, I cannot say that my research proposal was acceptable to all the officials in the Ministry of Education, some of whom had the traditional mind-set and intent on bureaucracy. They raised questions and concerns about the expenses and they did everything to get us entangled in administrative red tape.

However, Shaikh Hasan Al Al-Shaikh overcame every obstacle that came our way. He agreed to endorse and financially support the entire research project, provided me with a station wagon as my means of transport, and gave me an official letter addressed to the governors of the different regions of the Kingdom, asking them to assist me in the conduct of my research in any way they can.

I spent four months travelling in my station wagon, visiting several regions, such as Al-Summan, Al-Kharj, Wadi Fatima, the mountains of Al-Shafa, Al-Qatif, Al-Hasa, and Turabat Al-Baqum.

I finally decided on the topic of my research: a comparative study of the health of children in three different communities: a village, a hijrah (newly established Bedouin settlement), and a nomadic Bedouin community. The aim was to determine if there were any differences in the health of children of the three communities and what the causes of these differences might be. The only decision left was to find an area in the Kingdom where all three communities would be found living.

I still remember visiting a small village, Al-Hayathem in Al-Kharj; I can never forget this. I was with Shaikh Abdullah bin Raddas, a representative of the Ministry of Labor and Social Affairs. He was familiar with the region and the tribes who lived there, and he was well versed in their culture. The Shaikh of Al-Hayathem was away travelling, so we were received by his son. I stayed in Al-Hayathem for three days, investigating the health status of the children and the possible environmental impacts on their health.

Several weeks after that first visit, I returned to Al-Hayathem to gather more data. This time, I met Shaikh Khalid bin Hashr himself. He was a true Bedouin Shaikh, with rugged facial features exuding chivalry and masculinity, and eyes that revealed a natural shrewdness.

Shaikh Khalid welcomed me and asked the purpose of my visit.

I said, "I am a doctor conducting research, and I need to collect some information and statistics on health in the region. I am hopeful that the findings of my research will be of benefit to the people of this area."

He looked at me long and hard and said, "Listen, doctor, if you are telling me that you are here to write a report for the government to help us, we have no need for you here. On the other hand, if you are here to conduct a study that will help you gain a higher degree in medicine, then we will help you in any way possible, and you are most welcome among us."

The Shaikh's words shook me to my core. I deeply appreciated his frankness, openness, and clarity. Thereafter, we developed a strong bond that has withstood the test of time.

Two months went by and I was still trekking around the Kingdom in my grey station wagon. The topic of my research was now clear to me, but one question remained unanswered. Where will I conduct it? One day, I went to see the Minister of Labor and Social Affairs, Shaikh Abdul Rahman Aba Al-Khail. We touched upon my uncertainty about the area for the field study.

His words were simple, ending weeks of indecision, presenting me with the perfect solution to my problem, "You will find no place better than Turaba to conduct your field work. In Turaba, you will find nomadic Bedouins, newly settled Bedouins and the villagers living side by side. In the village of Turaba, the Social Development Center will be a suitable setting for your clinic and lab as well as a station for you and your team. He added, "We will make all the living arrangements for you and your family for the entire duration of your stay for the research."

The Minister wrote a letter of recommendation addressed to the director of the Social Development Center, requesting him to make all resources of the center available for my use.

I went to Turaba for a short exploratory visit accompanied by a guide assigned to me by the governor of Taif. The guide was skilled and experienced. His job was to show me around and introduce me to the Shaikh of Turaba.

There I was, on my way to Turaba to conduct the field work for my Dr. PH, which was unprecedented in the country. I was filled with energy and fervor, eager to apply what I had learned in university, but also filled with apprehension. I was out of my comfort zone, the academic environment in America in which I had been cocooned; without my colleagues, my professors, the library, and the laboratories.

Where do I start? What will I find in my research? How will the people of Turaba receive me? Whom would I talk to if I need help? Whom would I turn to if I run into difficulty?

These questions were revolving around my head as we wound our way up the mountain, overlooking the Turaba village and the few settlements surrounding it. Despite my anxiety over the enormous task ahead of me, I firmly believed in my heart that Allah would provide me with His help.

My exploratory visit to Turaba lasted over a week. I investigated the health status of a small sample of the children and collected some basic data on the health knowledge, attitudes and practices of the people in the three adjacent communities: the Nomadic Bedouins, the newly settled Bedouins and the villagers.

I needed a map of the region to find my way around, but there was no map available. I called on some of the older residents of Turaba who were familiar with the area; they came up with one name, Al-Shareef Muhammad bin Ali, an illiterate but very knowledgeable in the history and geography of Turaba.

On a large, white piece of paper, I made a sketch of the landscape of Turaba. The locals provided answers to the questions I asked and together we sketched out a map. There stood Mount Hidn, which separated Nejd from Hejaz. There is an old saying, "whoever has seen Mount Hidn has crossed over to Nejd". And there is Wadi Turaba, running from the South to the North dotted with several villages, small settlements, and houses. The settlement, Shaar, lay in the farthest north of Wadi Turaba, and Al-Khayala on the far south. Within a short time we had drawn ourselves a map of Al-Baqum. Although the map was nothing professional, it served its purpose.

My days were spent moving from village to village, between settlements, and Bedouin tents, meeting with the leaders of the different tribes, farmers, and Bedouin families. The pages of my daily journal were soon filled with all the information I could gather about life in Turaba: demographics, health services, sources of food, the names of the tribes and settlements, the houses of the Bedouins, the culture, the traditions, and lifestyle associated with health. Life there had its share of complexities and contradictions.

On one of our treks to a settlement from where we were, the station wagon caused sandy swirls behind us as we drove up the slopes in the desert. We were stopped by a Bedouin on the side of the path. He asked if we could give him a ride to his clan. When he found out that we were visitors to the area, he insisted on taking us to his home for a meal. We declined the invitation politely and tried to convince him that we had a task we needed to get to. He reluctantly accepted our excuse and let us go. On our way back later that afternoon, we saw him standing on the side of the path, holding a sheep. He told us that he would like to slaughter the sheep and have it cooked for a meal for us. Otherwise we should accept it as a gift from him and take it with us.

May Allah send you blessings and all that is good, Shaikh Manahi, for your generosity and kindness. Years later, this man visited me in my home in Riyadh, but I was unable to reciprocate his generosity with the simplicity and the spontaneity he had shown us that afternoon in Turaba.

On one of our journeys, we visited a small settlement to explore the possibility of including it in our study. I sat in a tent and started collecting information. Coffee was poured and a tray of dates was passed around. After I recorded the names and ages of about 30 children, I noticed the men around me were exchanging discreet glances with one another and whispering.

The eldest of them looked me in the eye and said, "Zohair, there is something I have to tell you. You seem to be a good man with no guile. We will not accuse you of betraying our trust. Now, you have become one of us. The names we gave earlier of the children were all false. Let me give you the correct names now."

He then disclosed the real names of the thirty children and I quickly wrote them down.

The mark of a Bedouin man is his instinctive native intelligence; the desert has taught him caution. The newly settled Bedouins are uncomfortable with complete strangers and unable to trust them at first. However, after an hour of chatting and sharing coffee and dates, they had felt reassured that I had no bad intentions.

I made my decision: Turaba would be the right place for my field work. At its center is a village, encircled by smaller settlements, and some Bedouin tents scattered here and there in the desert. I jotted down my objectives, the possible sample size of children to be studied, and the facilities and resources I required.

I returned to Taif to inform the authorities in the Ministries of Education, Health, Labor, and Social Affairs of my plan of work for the study. While waiting for the administrative work to be completed, I received a letter from my supervisor, Timothy Baker, advising me to spend a couple of weeks at Aramco Hospital in Dhahran, to prepare for my laboratory work before heading back to the USA.

Aramco Hospital agreed to my four- week stay with them at the recommendation of the Deputy Minister of the Ministry of Petroleum and Mineral Resources, Hisham Nazer. It was the month of Ramadan. My monthly stipend of SR 1,000 from the Ministry of Education was not going to be enough to cover travel expenses to celebrate the Eid holiday with my family in Makkah, so I had to spend the Eid in Dhahran.

I busied myself with work. I had to write a report of all the information I had collected in Turaba for submission to the university in the United States. I estimated that I would need a few days with no distractions, completely on my own to finish the report. I could find no better, more peaceful place than Tarout Island, just off the coast of Dammam, to devote my entire time to writing the report. I took all my papers and my portable typewriter, and there at the small local hospital on Tarout Island, I typed the findings of my exploratory visit to Turaba and the preparations I had made at Aramco Hospital.

It was time to return to my university in Baltimore, but the university had arranged for me to stop in several countries on my way back to the US. I was to visit Pakistan, India, Taiwan, Thailand, and Japan to investigate the healthcare systems these countries had in place for their rural populations. These travels lasted three weeks. My family and I were privileged to meet some very kind people who worked in our embassies in the different countries we visited. They took care of my wife and daughter while I went on visits to the health centers in the rural areas.

These visits opened my eyes to a variety of healthcare practices in Asia and Far East. My examination confirmed that the most important contributory influences on the health of the individual and the society are not the healthcare systems available. Rather, they are the socioeconomic status of the individual, which is linked to the person's income, living conditions, diet, and education. It became clear to me that doctors may excel at treating diseases, but the impact of the health services on improving the overall health of a society would be minimal unless doctors and other members of the healthcare team were schooled in preventive measures during their medical school training and after graduation. Only a few doctors receive such fundamental instruction.

Upon graduating, doctors and other allied healthcare personnel are capable of treating the patient's illness, but are not equipped to prevent disease before it strikes.

Changes need to be made in the education system of medical schools, both in the content and teaching methods. The role of doctors and healthcare personnel should include prevention, improvement of overall health and treatment. Modern medicine must become more comprehensive to take cognizance of the relationship between health and the environment. What we need is a holistic approach to medicine that focuses on the whole person: body, mind, and soul, in sickness and in health.

I pause here to reflect on some things that I witnessed in Japan, and how I came to the realization that a civilization is to be viewed as a whole and should not be divided into its individual parts. My Japanese escort led me to a health center in a small village on the outskirts of Tokyo. Before stepping into the health center, patients would remove their shoes and wear indoor slippers. I looked around. There was not a single piece of paper on the floor, no cigarette butts, nor any sign of carelessness. Everything was clean and orderly and pleasing to the eye. There were even vases of flowers in several corners of the center!

I asked my escort to take me to any of the houses in the village for me to take a look at the sanitation. He hesitated for a moment, which confirmed what I had heard and read about the Japanese people, that they were not keen on letting a complete stranger into their homes. Suddenly, my escort offered that I visit his home. His wife greeted us at the door. As she showed me around the house, I once again came to the conclusion that a civilization is a whole that cannot be broken down into its individual parts. It was a small house with a miniature garden. Every corner of the house exhibited cleanliness and elegance. Again there were flowers everywhere. While sipping a cup of tea, my escort introduced me to his son, a twelve-year-old boy. I asked the boy what his hobbies were, and he replied that he was interested in astronomy. I did not take his answer seriously. What could a young boy know about astronomy? My initial skepticism quickly turned into admiration when he showed me maps of the stars that he had drawn. He led me to their backyard to show me his telescope. I developed great respect for Japanese culture.

Back to Baltimore, and in the following eight months I finalized preparations for my field work, composed the questionnaires for my study, and made a list of all the blood tests and medical examinations I would administer. I arranged with the Centers for Disease Control in Atlanta, Georgia, for the blood samples to be sent frozen in small containers from Turaba to their laboratories for serological tests. The university allocated $50,000 for the purchase of the necessary equipment for the research. Since I wanted to start my research the next summer, we were very pressed for time, so I had to work around the clock to meet that deadline.

I will digress here because I feel compelled to tell the story of my professor, Dr. Carl Tyler, the Chairman of the Department of International Health at Johns Hopkins University. His story, his way of life and his perseverance are worth contemplating. On more than one occasion, I invited him to visit Saudi Arabia when I became the director of planning and programming in the Ministry of Health in Riyadh. I learned a great deal from Carl Tyler. He was exemplary in his knowledge and dedication to his work. He played a key role in teaching hundreds of public health professionals all over the world.

Every few years, he would take a year off work at the university and go to a developing nation to implement measures for disease prevention in places where he thought the people would benefit the most. He would return to the university a year later, having acquired even more experience and knowledge which he used to further enrich his teaching and research.

Once, the Indian government invited him to study the phenomenon that made most Indian doctors so reluctant to work in the rural areas. Carl Tyler, together with his wife and children, packed their bags and headed to India to live for a year. He insisted on living in a rural area for the entire year, despite all attempts by the officials of the Ministry of Health to persuade him not to. He did not yield. His reasoning was that, if he was in India to study the problems that doctors in the rural areas faced, then he would live there too and experience first-hand their hardships and challenges. The health authorities from the ministry tried to change Tyler's mind through his wife, but she would not betray her husband's trust. He got what he wanted. He rented a humble home in the village where he resided with his family.

Carl Tyler spared no effort in making a pleasing home out of the house he rented. He cleaned out his yard and placed screens in all the windows to keep mosquitoes out. He built a water tank at the bottom and on the roof of the house. He re-painted the whole house both on the inside and outside, and planted a garden of beautiful flowers in the yard. In a matter of weeks, and at a reasonable cost, he had transformed the house into an attractive sight, a landmark for the village and neighboring villages as well.

Carl Tyler was among the first to call for global enhancement of primary healthcare. Hundreds of medical students studied and trained under his leadership, who then continued their work in improving public health all over the world.

A new dean who was appointed to the Johns Hopkins School of Public Health at the university, did not believe in Tyler's ideas of primary healthcare and the holistic approach to healthcare, and wanted to steer the School in a different direction. News spread like wildfire of these impending changes, and Professor Carl Tyler's former students now living in all corners of the globe heard the news too. Tyler's students sent hundreds of letters to the university, inundating the university administrators with correspondence, objecting to this change. The university was compelled to give in to these objections and retain Professor Tyler's ideas.

Until recently, until they passed away, I visited my professors Carl Tyler and Timothy Baker whenever I went to the United States. Even when Carl Tyler turned seventy years, he still rode his bicycle from his house in the suburbs of Baltimore to the university in the downtown area. The last time I went to see him, though in his eighties, he was sitting at his computer desk typing a paper.

By June 1967, I had completed all the preparations for my research. Everything was carefully planned and organized, and things were in place for our move to Saudi Arabia.

All of a sudden, politics turned events around, and there were ominous dark clouds over the Middle Eastern skies. Military action began over the

Suez Canal in Egypt. War broke out in the region, and the media started disseminating news that Arabs were hostile towards Israel, a small, peaceful country that was a friend of the West. People in America wished for the defeat of the so-called Arab rogue states. Their eyes seemed blind, their ears deaf, and their hearts closed to the truth. This is an example of media influence on public opinion: what people think. It demonstrates that sheer power can be so loud that it drowns the voice of truth and justice.

As for us Arab students in the US, we were forced to lower our heads as we walked in silence, our hearts bleeding. The discrimination we felt in Baltimore became unbearable for my family and me, so we went to New York to wait for tempers to cool down. But in New York, we were surrounded by the Jewish community. Mockery and racial slurs followed us everywhere. We returned to Baltimore when the crisis in the Middle East began to settle, but nothing was resolved.

My supervisor, Timothy Baker, said to me, "Go ahead and travel to Saudi Arabia. If you find the atmosphere suitable for the conduct of the research, send me a telegram with a note saying: the car is ready. In which case, I will follow you to supervise your research."

The other supervisor, the anthropologist, apologized and withdrew his offer to go with us to Saudi Arabia.

Chapter 5

Turabat Al-Baqum

I traveled to the Kingdom in the middle of the summer of 1967 to begin my field work. I took all the laboratory equipment that I needed, which the university had purchased. Upon my arrival, I discovered that I had been living in an ivory tower. It was now time for me to come down into the real world and learn of matters of life that I had not been taught in the university.

The customs officer in Jeddah wanted to stop me from my bringing in the laboratory equipment, asking if the tools were for commercial purposes.

"By Allah, the only purpose for bringing this laboratory equipment is to examine children," I said.

Nevertheless, the customs officials said he wanted to have an inventory, a record of every piece of equipment I had with me, and bank statements, and fill out at least ten different forms; otherwise, the equipment would not be allowed to pass through customs. All the effort and time spent dealing with customs and completing the paperwork would have been better off spent in my field work.

What occurred at the university in America put this situation in sharp relief. After the university approved the purchase of medical devices and equipment, the board members of the Department of International Health went away to a conference out of the city. Acting in their absence as the administrator was an American colleague of mine who was also preparing a Dr.PH dissertation. He signed the check to the amount of $50,000 for me to purchase the equipment and devices and at a time when $50,000 was a great deal of money. The whole transaction took no longer than an hour.

On the subject of complicated administrative procedures that we all deal with at one time or another in the Arab world, another story comes to mind, the story of Dr. Greep, the Dean of the College of Medicine at Maastricht University in Holland. A few years ago, I went to see him at the university and he invited me to lunch.

We were sitting on the terrace of the restaurant when he pointed to a building in the distance and asked, "Do you remember that building?"

"Isn't that the building of the College of Medicine where you were before you moved into the new buildings?" I asked.

"Yes, I sold that building," he said.

"You sold it?" I asked, intrigued.

"Yes. After we moved into the new buildings, I was approached by a Japanese delegation. They wanted to purchase that building. They stated their offer, which I took to the President of the university. He accepted the offer. I oversaw the procedure and until the sale was finalized," said Dr. Greep.

I asked, "How long did the whole process take?"

"Two weeks," he replied.

I was speechless, but tried to hide my astonishment.

These nations were able to make enormous strides in their economy and industry because of the great importance they put on time. They value time. They do away with most of the bureaucratic procedures that drain us of time. Instead, they adopt a more dynamic and pro-active method of planning, implementing, follow up, and evaluating in their administrative process.

In the 1980s, the book, "The One Minute Manager", became widely popular; over 8 million copies were printed in several languages. The book advocated utilizing every single minute in business management. That idea became popular two decades ago. The most recent book published on a similar notion is called "The Ten Second Internet Manager". I expect that a new book called "The One Second Manager" will soon be in print.

It was not only the situation at Jeddah customs that brought me back down to the real world, but several other incidents. I must testify that although I had a very rough time, I learned many lessons.

The Minister of Education, Shaikh Hasan Al Al-Shaikh, issued an order for me to be provided with a car for three months, so that my research team and I could get around in Turaba. However, the proponents of strict bureaucratic procedures doubted the legitimacy of the Minister's order I had. They thought that according to the financial regulations such expenditure was considered a waste of the country's wealth. Allah sent me someone to solve my problem: Mustafa Attar, the Director of the Department of Education in Makkah, who later became a close friend. He granted me the use of a car, under his responsibility.

Next, I went to the administrator of Al-Zahir Hospital in Makkah with a letter from the Minister of Health, requesting him to assign a nurse to accompany me on my field work in Turaba. The hospital administrator called a non-Saudi nurse and informed her that she was to go with me to Turaba to do some field work.

She smiled and said, "At your service."

The minute the hospital administrator stepped out of the room, she whirled around and hissed, "Listen, doctor, I swear by Allah Who has made the Prophet a prophet, if you take me with you to Turaba, you will regret it. I will show you stars in daylight!"

Stunned by her reaction, all I had the strength to do was to invoke the mercy of Allah to descend upon me, seek refuge in Allah, and ask for His help so that I could fulfill my mission.

The next morning, I received a phone call from the hospital administrator saying, "Dr. Zohair, a Saudi nurse came and reproached me for choosing someone other than her to accompany you on your field work. She said she was the daughter of this land and it was her duty to assist you on this mission."

Whenever her name is mentioned, I send up a prayer for her. Fatima Jamaan, may Allah bless you wherever you may be and wherever you may go, for your goodwill and greatness.

The Ministry of Labor and Social Affairs assigned four social workers to my research team in Turaba. The Ministry of Health provided me with a nurse, laboratory technician, and a surveyor. My wife also joined the team, making our team a total of eight people. We began the initial stages of the preparations for the research. I sent a telegram to my supervisor, Dr. Baker, at the university in the United States saying, "The car is ready." He would understand this message.

Two more steps needed to be taken before my supervisor would come from the United States and before we begin the field work. The first was to obtain permission from His Royal Highness Prince Fahad bin Abdul Aziz (later King Fahad), the Minister of Interior, to conduct my research in Turaba. Second, I needed a detailed accurate map of the region.

I went to see His Royal Highness Prince Fahd in his office in Jeddah. After a brief but enjoyable chat with him about the research, its goals, and usefulness to society, he gave me permission to begin the field work. However, he warned me about the extreme temperatures of Turaba in the month of August. Driven by the enthusiasm of youth, I was unwilling to succumb to any obstacles, be they the sweltering heat or the bitter cold.

I went to the Ministry of Petroleum and Mineral Resources where my friend Fouad Abbas Kattan gave me the only map they had of Turaba. However, I found the map incomplete. I requested a meeting with the Minister himself, Shaikh Ahmed Zaki Yamani. I explained the purpose of my research, and why I needed an accurate map of the region. I suggested that I take aerial pictures of the region. The minister agreed and instructed that I should be taken by helicopter to Turaba.

With the help of the engineer Saeed Farsi, we flew by a helicopter to Turaba to take aerial pictures of the landscape. The people of Turaba were surprised to see this auspicious metal bird hovering over their heads, making a thunderous noise. The arrival of the helicopter made history that day in Turaba. The day the helicopter flew over their heads became a reference point in their history used to mark dates for the births and deaths of people in Turaba, just as the great flood a few years earlier, and the skirmishes between the two tribes, Wazi' and Mahameed had been used.

I greeted my professor on his arrival at Jeddah airport, and I drove us both to Turaba, passing through Taif on our way. When we were halfway between Jeddah and Makkah, I noticed that he had become suddenly quiet. He was no longer paying attention to what I was saying. He seemed to be in another spiritual realm. He asked me to remain quiet.

Later, when I asked him what happened he said, "A strange feeling came over me as we were nearing Makkah. Something disconnected me from reality and lifted me far away to God's Kingdom."

No doubt, what my professor felt was a strong pull, a return to the natural instinctive belief in the One God. If we called people to Islam in a beautiful way, many people who are lost would find the peace and sanctuary that comes with having faith in Allah.

During the short few hours that we spent on the trip, climbing up towards Taif, my professor and I went over the goals of my research, procedure, equipment, methods, and the obstacles that I had encountered so far and those still expected. My professor's advice was to firmly adhere to the goals and objectives of the research. However, on the matter of the method and procedure, he said to be flexible and adapt to our circumstances, the available resources, cultural beliefs, and the receptiveness of the society.

My professor's advice was very helpful, and I remembered his wise words when I later ran into difficult situations that almost halted my research. On one occasion, I was surprised when parents in Turaba refused to allow me to draw blood samples (only 10 ml) of their children,. Rumors had spread among Turaba residents that based on the results of the blood tests some of their sons would be recruited for the military. Another rumor that caught on was that we were adding blood to our tea, to give us strength and vigor. They felt their suspicions confirmed because we drank a lot of hot tea, even more than we drank water!

To stop the rumors, I was forced to change the way I conducted the tests, in order not to create any superstitions. Instead of drawing blood samples in small tubes, we only pricked the children's fingers to collected a few droplets of blood to test for hemoglobin and malaria parasites.

On our drive to Turaba, we stopped for a few hours in Taif, where we met the Director of the Department of Health Affairs, Dr. Abdul Karim Bakhsh. When I told Dr. Bakhsh that I had been looking for a scale to measure infants' weight, but had not found any on the market in Jeddah, he remembered that he had one in the storeroom. He promptly gave it to us to take to Turaba.

Our final stop was Turabat Al-Baqum, and more specifically the Social Development Center, where we were stationed. It was a spacious, two story building, the top floor of which we used as the residence for the research team. On the bottom floor, we set up the clinics, laboratory, an exam room for taking anthropometric measurements, and a medical records room.

My family and I took up a large room for our residence. We furnished it with whatever simple furniture we found at the Social Development Center warehouse. Our room was multi-functional: in that room we ate, slept, relaxed, and it was where our three-year-old daughter, Sahar, played. For the research team, there was a suite for the women and one for the men. My supervisor from the US had his private living area, where he stayed for two weeks. Although our living quarters were cramped, we were untroubled and did not complain. Everyone working in our research center was accommodating and interested in the wellbeing and comfort of the other.

I want to share with my readers the purpose and the goal of the research. I started with the hypothesis that there were no discrepancies in the health status of children living in the three different societies in Turaba: the village, settlement, and Bedouin tents. I formulated this hypothesis after my initial exploration of Turaba, as I had observed no disparity in the health awareness and lifestyles of the residents of the three different communities. Moreover, the health center in the village (mostly available for the village inhabitants) seemed to have no apparent impact on disease prevention or improvement of the overall health of the villagers.

My task was to either confirm or refute the hypothesis. The end result was not the main concern. What was most important was the methodology I would use to collect and analyze data, and how I would obtain results from the data collected. The methodology and the process of studying, research, planning, and the field work were to take two years. This was to put me on the first rung of the ladder up my own scientific research and the attainment of a Dr. PH degree. I was taking the initial steps on the road to scientific research, the end of which was still far off. In fact, this road never truly ends.

For three months, we all worked very hard collecting information from people in the village, settlements, and Bedouin areas; we worked as collaborative team. Our study covered five areas in Turaba: Souq, Kara, Ergain, Jebail, and Alawa. We studied the environment, diet, health knowledge, beliefs, attitudes, and financial status of the families. We also conducted a physical exam in the clinic for children below five years of age and took their anthropometric measurements. We collected specimens of blood, urine, and stool. We ran the tests that were feasible in our small laboratory and sent samples of serum for further investigations in the laboratories of the Centers for Disease Control in Atlanta, Georgia in the United States.

We worked round the clock for two weeks, and took two days off to spend in Taif so that the team members could relax. During those short breaks, I took care of the necessary administrative work, with the ministries of Health, Education, and Social Affairs.

For the success of our field work, it was imperative for us to earn the trust of the people in Turaba. We needed to gain the trust of the governors of the region, the tribal leaders, and those holding important administrative positions in government. Every time we met people, and every time someone new came to our clinic, we took the opportunity to explain the purpose of the research. One after another, we received countless invitations to lunch or dinner in the homes of the generous, hospitable people of Turaba. While we enjoyed a meal together, the relaxed atmosphere made it easy to talk and elaborate on the purpose of our research.

We found this communication between us and the people of Turaba extremely useful for the progress of our research. Their willingness to cooperate with us was slow in coming, but that is understandable because the presence of both men and women in our research team was something the people were unaccustomed to and unusual in their conservative society. It is perfectly normal that not everyone would be on the same level of acceptance of the idea behind our research. However, after some explanation, they welcomed the idea and came on board. Some people even invited us to build a hospital in their village. The presence of medical staff and researchers, to many people, meant that a hospital was to be established.

When sharing a meal with the people of Turaba, they opened their hearts to us. Their all-time favorite topic at the dinner table was marriage. Endless conversations revolved around the same question: why did I settle for only one wife? Did I wish to marry a second wife? If I was interested in marrying again, could they help provide me with a suitable wife? There was one obstacle though, my family name. I was from the family of Sebai, not Sebaie; my family was not a tribal family. They even offered to help my supervisor find a suitable wife. That was until they found out that he was Christian. This discovery caused an outcry and all offers were withdrawn.

We had just two weeks to the end of our time there, for my supervisor and I to finalize all preparations for the field work. We needed to revise the goals of the research, procedures, check the laboratory equipment, train the staff (men and women), and explore the villages, settlements, and Bedouin tents. In the evenings, we hunched together over the map of Turaba and the pictures I had taken from the helicopter to determine the locations of the field work.

The day before my supervisor's departure, we were faced with an unanticipated problem. A group of young men who had been sent by one of the ministries to work in the area, took up residence in the Social Development Center. At the time, we were still in the wake of the six-day June 1967 war in which Israel had encroached upon more lands and killed around 20,000 Arab men of the Egyptian forces, Jordanians and Palestinians. When the young men from the ministries realized that my supervisor was American, they became openly hostile towards him. To them, he was the epitome of imperialism and colonialism. They verbally abused him, criticizing US foreign policy, accused him of being complicit to his government's policies, and threatened him.

My supervisor was in an awkward situation; a stranger in the midst of a group of angry young men. I tried to calm them down. I tried to convince the leader of their delegation that my supervisor did not represent the US government. I explained that he came to Turaba to help me with my scientific research, which would be of benefit and value to our dear country. I told them that I was studying in the US, that I had been safe and the people there treated me well, but all my arguments were to no avail. Their leader still bristled with rage, and his hostility would soon turn into physical aggression against my supervisor. At that critical moment, I remembered the letter I had from the Ministry of Interior. I rushed and got the letter and read it to them. The letter stated that my supervisor, Professor Baker, was to accompany me for my field work, and it was everyone's responsibility to cooperate and assist the research team, to ensure the success of this research in Turaba. After I had read the letter, it was as if I had just poured cold water over their heads; their temper cooled and they withdrew.

The women in my team collected information from over 300 families in the villages, settlements, and Bedouin tents in Turaba. They inquired about the health status of mothers and children, nutrition, pregnancy, birth, breastfeeding and weaning, and the children's nutrition. Each female member of our team had one of the village women to escort her. They rode together in a pick-up truck to visit the different homes and tents. It was in the middle of August. You can imagine the heat in that region in mid -August. Every evening, the women stayed up to document and analyze the data they had collected.

The social workers' job was to interview the men in the various households and collect information on the social and economic status of the family, the environment, the sources of their drinking water and nutrition.

My lab technician, together with a health inspector took the blood samples and got other body fluid samples from the children. They also measured the height and weight of the children, and collected samples of the drinking water for testing.

In addition to having general oversight of all processes of the field work, I conducted physical exams of the children in my clinic, and ran laboratory tests. Every evening, I met with my research team to go over the information we had gathered and plan for the next day.

I have many stories to tell of the dedication and the devotion of the research team to the work in hand. The unrelenting hard work of each member of my research team was truly inspiring. One of these stories is of a woman, a research assistant who had been assigned to stay with us for only three weeks, and was expected to return to the hospital she worked for in Jeddah. She left, but to our surprise she returned a few days later, with her husband! She said, "I found myself in the hospital in Jeddah sitting comfortably in an air-conditioned office, and all I could think of was you all working day and night in these difficult conditions. I asked my superiors to send me back to Turaba. In any case, I thought if they did not agree to my request, I would come anyway."

To this day, I pray for her, Mrs. Shami, for Allah to protect her and reward her.

Not only did we collect health information from the inhabitants of Turaba, but we also provided health services such as immunization for children and health education programs for the families. Admittedly, we had difficulties, and it is only by the grace and help of Allah that we successfully completed our work.

There is one difficult incident I will never forget. One day one of the men came running into my office, begging me to help. His wife was giving birth, but there seemed to be complications and the doctor in charge of the Health Center was not available. It was Friday (the weekend) and the doctor was in Taif. I took a nurse with me to the man's house. His wife had already given birth, but the placenta was still in the uterus. This was a critical life-threatening situation for the mother. Manually removing the placenta could cause heavy blood loss which would be difficult to control with our limited medical facilities. She needed immediate hospital attention. The nurse and I provided first aid and arranged for her to be taken to the hospital in Taif.

A little later, I was informed that the woman had not been taken to Taif. Her husband and family were keeping her at home hoping that relief would come and the placenta would detach by itself. I was left with no other option but to attempt, against all medical protocol, to manually remove the placenta with the help of the nurse. By the mercy of Allah, the patient did not hemorrhage and she was saved from imminent death. This incident and others like it created a bond between us, the researchers and the families of Turaba.

Fortunately, at the time, the Minister of Education, Shaikh Hasan Al Al-Shaikh, was also the Minister of Health. He believed in the value of our work and gave us his full support.

I went to him in his office every two weeks with multiple requirements. Our needs included materials for the children's immunizations, expenses for fuel for the car, and a request for the extension of the assignment of our team members. I wrote down my requests which he graciously signed immediately.

Some insights into the culture and the environment of Turaba as it was then can be found in excerpts from my book *Family Health in Turabat Al-Baqum*.

Remember that I speak of the society in Turaba in the late 1960s. No doubt, drastic social, economic, and cultural changes have occurred in Turaba since I did my field work.

"Turaba has a deeply-rooted rich culture as some artifacts of clay utensils discovered there date back thousands of years to the pre-Islamic period. Because of its strategic position at the foot of Mount Hidn, which lies between Nejd and Hejaz, Turaba was often the field for many battles. The last of the wars in this region was the conflict between King Abdul Aziz's forces inching their way westward from Nejd, and the Hashimi forces in Turaba. The victory of the Saudi forces in Turaba was decisive. It opened the way for King Abdul Aziz's forces to advance to Taif and the remaining areas of Hejaz.

Most of the residents of Turaba are descendants of the Al-Baqum tribe, one of the oldest and largest tribes in the Kingdom. Al-Baqum is made up of two groups: Wazi' and Mahameed.

Chapter 6

Back to America

I returned to the United States, carrying with me three large boxes filled with over 300 files of all the information we had gathered in the study in Turaba. That same amount of information today could have been stored on a couple CDs which would easily fit into a jacket pocket.

I went back to work at the university in my small office with a window overlooking the intersection of Wolf St. and Washington St. in Baltimore city. With my wife's help, I started analyzing, logging, and organizing all the data we had collected, and I began writing my research proposal.

Our last year in America was a bit more relaxed and enjoyable. As a researcher, I received a stipend from the university. Apart from working on my dissertation, there were not many lectures to attend, which gave us more time to broaden our horizons. We finally had time for entertainment and social activities.

We stocked up on camping necessities: a small tent, cooking utensils, sleeping bags, and other basics and arranged a schedule of weekend camping trips. We went to the Maryland countryside and some of the neighboring states. We spent our nights in a forest under the trees beside a river, or by a lake. These short trips were delightful and inexpensive, and gave us a taste of American outdoor life.

It took over a year to analyze the data that we had recorded in Turaba and review the results of the laboratory tests performed at the Centers for Disease Control in Georgia. We used a computer to analyze and draw graphs of the data. Before the advent of today's compact PC and laptops, the computer we used was bulky and took up practically a whole room.

Public Health Study

This book is not the place to discuss the results of my study in detail, since this information has been previously published in my book entitled, 'Family Health in a Changing Arab Society". In summary, it would suffice to say that my study in 1967 revealed several health problems in Turaba' s society, most of which were the result of environmental and lifestyle factors. In my visit to the area 15 years later, I found some improvement in the health status of the society. This improvement in health status was due more to the rise in the people's income, education, and nutrition than to the development of the healthcare services in the area.

I completed my dissertation under the supervision of my professor, Timothy Baker. My professor had only a Master's degree, but a person's merit and wealth of knowledge cannot be measured by a degree or certificate. When I told him that the brilliant writer, Abbas Al-Aqqad had no more than elementary schooling, my professor's face lit up with a confident satisfied smile.

I submitted my dissertation. A few days after submission, I had to come before a panel of judges to discuss my research. The panel comprised scientists, university's professors, and external examiners. The judges could decide to approve the dissertation or ask me to rewrite it, or reject it altogether, in which case I would have to conduct the research all over. All that was left was to wait for the day of the viva voce. While waiting, I took the opportunity to spend some time in solitude to think. I asked myself: *What was my research about? What was my plan for the future? What had I learnt from the whole experience?*

Certainly, I had taken the first step in the process of scientific research. I had learned the scientific research methodology and procedures, which were important skills to acquire. I had discovered firsthand the health status and healthcare services available in my country. Working on my dissertation helped me hone my writing skills. More and more, I appreciated the value of time and being organized.

I learned much about human nature; the research opened my eyes to different people with differing personalities. Among the people I met were some who nothing could make happier than help and serve other people, expecting nothing in return, not even a word of thanks. There were others whom, nothing made more miserable than another's success. I met people who absolutely could not lie or deceive; who by nature were so open and principled that they would do nothing that went against those principles. Still, there were those who would never speak the truth; to them telling the truth was an onerous task, it was like climbing a high mountain. On being given a task, there were those who would do what is asked of them and nothing more; there were those who would not even perform the tasks they are meant to do, and then there were those who would go well beyond the call of duty; they would go that extra mile working to their full capacity.

The time came to defend my dissertation, and I found myself in front of five evaluating professors. The discussion lasted three hours, and the judges' decision was announced. I had passed; my dissertation was approved, all praise and thanks to Allah. Today, if someone asked me whom I would dedicate my doctorate dissertation, without a moment's hesitation my answer would be; my wife. She patiently strove and struggled with me, seeking a reward only from Allah. My wife supported and helped me. She encouraged me to believe in myself and even in the most difficult times, convincing me to continue my research in spite of all the odds against me.

We had only three weeks before we were to leave the United States. In those three weeks, I had to finalize the publication of my research paper, and close the tenancy of our accommodation in Baltimore. I wanted to take a few days to study the health status of the children in a Native American community. I wanted to visit the Centers for Disease Control in Atlanta, Georgia. I also planned to attend a medical conference in Detroit. My university helped to arrange the visit to Detroit to attend the conference.

I flew to Atlanta, Georgia, and was greeted at the airport by a representative from the Centers for Disease Control, who was to show me around, and organize my visit to the center. On our way to the hotel, he mentioned that he was a member of a religious organization whose mission it was to call the youth to return to the teachings of Jesus. He asked if I would like to join their meeting later on in the evening and listen to a lecture by a priest; he was going to speak about Jesus Christ (peace be upon him).

I welcomed the idea and I went to the meeting with him. He drove up to an exquisite mansion. In a spacious room, I found around thirty young men and women sitting on cushions scattered around, listening intently to the priest telling them about Jesus.

The priest was saying, "Jesus came to call people to love, peace, and goodness. If we believe in the Bible and we believe that Jesus is our savior, we are guaranteed entry into Paradise."

After the lecture, I approached the priest and warmly thanked him for the lecture.

I asked the priest, "I believe in Jesus (peace be upon him) and I believe that he is a prophet of God, and I believe in his mother, Virgin Mary, but my belief is based on a source other than the Bible. The source of my knowledge and faith is from the Holy Qur'an, will I still have a place in Paradise?"

He took an inquisitive look at me and vigorously shook his head, "No!"

After my short stay in Atlanta, I traveled to Arizona to study the health services in a Native American reservation, of the Red Indian Navaho tribe. The Red Indians have a great civilization and a long history in America. Most of the movies we watch at the cinema about Red Indians are a distortion of history. I stayed in the Native American reservation for three days. The people lived in small houses, widely dispersed in the desert. Their lives were different from those of the average white American. Some of the elders could not speak English. The children were sent to modern boarding schools where they stayed and studied all week and only returned home to their families for the weekends.

At school, the children learnt to be competitive, independent, and impatient while at home their culture promoted cooperation, working together, and relaxation. The children grew up torn between these two conflicting social environments. After graduation, the young adults move into bigger cities to look for work in the job market, often living in isolated neighborhoods along with other minorities of the American society. A large percentage of them detest living in the city because they find them too crowded, busy, competitive, and stressful. Many of them return to their secluded communities. Owing to their internal struggles and the cultural gap between their community and white America, it is not uncommon for their youth to suffer an identity crisis. In Native American communities, there is high unemployment and alcohol addiction.

The situation for Native Americans may have changed over the past quarter of a century. The federal government has provided schools, hospitals, and public services for their communities but they are reluctant to make use of these services. And even when they do use any of the government's services, commitment and loyalty to their culture takes precedence over all else. When illness strikes, they visit the conventional doctor at the clinic but they also consult their traditional healer, who is called a medicine man/woman or shaman. Native Americans believe that their traditional method of healing is part of a rich, complex system of beliefs, rituals, and practices. When the sick recover from the illness, the recovery is attributed not to the doctor's medicine from the clinic, but to their own traditional medicine.

What I witnessed first-hand at the Red Indian reservation in Arizona, confirmed what I had read about and learned from experience in life; that the health of a society is more directly linked to that society's environment, education, culture, traditional beliefs and practices, and economic status than it is to the health services provided. The disparity in the levels of health between the Red Indian and the typical white American is due to the differences in the environment, educational background, and standard of living.

After my fascinating trip to Arizona, it was time for my wife and I to bid farewell to America, to Johns Hopkins University, to our acquaintances and friends. We have fond memories of the four years that we spent in Baltimore, despite the ups and downs of those four years.

We packed our bags and headed to the United Kingdom. Before returning to Saudi Arabia, I was scheduled to spend a few weeks as a locum physician at the teaching hospital in Edinburgh and in Lincoln. On the first day of our arrival in Lincoln we ran into a problem. The organizers at the hospital who had arranged my visit had assumed that I would be coming alone, and were surprised to see my family with me. They had a room reserved for me in the hospital housing, which was not appropriate for a family. They tried to find suitable accommodation for myself and my family in their small town, but were not successful. In the end, the only solution to this problem was for me to stay by myself in hospital accommodation and for my wife and daughter to stay at a convent for Catholic nuns. We had no other option.

This was a unique experience for my wife; a door was opened for her to experience a new, different, and definitely intriguing world. She had the opportunity to engage in endless conversations with the nuns about the two faiths, Islam and Christianity. They tried to win her over to the belief in Jesus Christ as the Savior and she tried to convert them to Islam, but neither side was able to convince the other. Their differences of opinion and conviction in no way spoiled the amicable relationship they had developed with each other in those few days that my wife stayed with them. They treated her with kindness and respect and cared for her as one of their own.

I still, think of Dr. Robinson, the Chief of Pediatrics at Lincoln Hospital with a lot of respect and admiration. He was an epitome of a doctor whose life was dedicated to medicine, the art of healing. His white coat with his stethoscope hung conveniently on the door to enable him, respond instantly when called in an emergency any time of the night. Within minutes of a phone call, he would have put on his coat, grabbed his stethoscope, and rushed to see the patient. He took pains to attend the autopsy of any of his patients who died to determine the cause of death and compare the previous diagnosis with the results of the postmortem examination. He wanted to find out if he had made any mistakes in the diagnosis of his patients.

Fishing was Dr. Robinson's hobby. One room in his house was filled with fishing equipment and supplies: fishing rods, nets, hooks, and more. Every weekend, he went with his friends on a fishing trip to a lake or river. At the end of their excursion, they would weigh all the fish they had caught, record it in a journal, and return the fish to the water.

I learned self-discipline and devotion to one's work from Dr. Robinson.

There was still a month to go to the end of my time as a locum physician in Lincoln when I received a telegram from my father. The message stated that my father was planning to travel to London for some medical tests. I cut my stay in Lincoln short so I could be with my father in London for his medical examination and treatment.

It was the late 1960s, the time of the emergence of the hippie movement in the United States and Europe. Hippies were predominantly young people who were opposed to the establishment, mainstream culture, and societal norms. Hippies called for harmony with nature, communal living, artistic experimentation particularly in music, vegetarianism, sexual liberation, and even the use of recreational drugs. Young men walked around with pierced ears, women with frizzy hair dyed in all colors of the rainbow, some of them barefoot, half naked, and their unwashed bodies emitting repulsive body odor.

In Trafalgar Square, a young man approached me and asked for a shilling to buy some food, saying that he was hungry. My father urged me to ask the young man to go to a barber to have his unruly hair trimmed.

The young man replied, "I will not bow my head down to a barber."

We gave him the shilling and we thought how ironic! Bowing his head to a barber would damage his pride, yet he would ask people for money rather than work and be able to hold his head high with dignity.

The day before our flight from London to Saudi Arabia was the 21st of September in the year 1969, the day a new page was turned in history. We watched as images on the television showed Neil Armstrong land on the moon, emerge out of his spacecraft and become the first person to set foot on the moon.

We heard him say his unforgettable line, "One small step for man, one giant leap for mankind."

We returned to the Kingdom to begin a new chapter in the story of my life.

Chapter 7

The Ministry of Health

I returned to the Kingdom after a twelve-year absence from my country studying and pursuing my education, first in Egypt and then in Germany, the United States, and the United Kingdom. I had been back to the Kingdom for the summers and other holidays, and for my research and field work. These had been short and intermittent visits during which I had felt more like a visitor or a guest than a son of the soil.

I left the Kingdom a 17- year old, and returned on the verge of turning thirty. When I left, I had minimal experience of life and even less knowledge. I came back a father and a doctor with a Bachelor's degree, a diploma, Master's degree, and a Dr. PH degree under my belt. I was filled with confidence and hope that I had become an important doctor, ready to improve the health of my society in the Kingdom, and protect the masses from disease. That was what I thought at the time, but the reality was that I was only at the initial stages of my career path. I had little experience in life, and I still had much to learn of the world of work. If I knew then what I know now, I would have kept my self-confidence in check, and spared myself a lot of heartache. However, that is the wisdom of Allah. He makes it possible for us to follow the path we were made for; that which matches our strengths and gifts.

My small family stayed back in Makkah while I went on to Riyadh to prepare for our new life there. It was a new stage in my life. I had completed my studies and it was time to work; time to put into practice what I had learned; time to become an agent of change in my society.

As soon as I arrived in Riyadh, I paid a visit to Shaikh Hasan Al al-Shaikh, who at the time held two important positions. He was the Minister of

Education and also served as the Acting Minister of Health. Shaikh Hasan Al al-Shaikh received me with the greatest warmth. He offered me two choices: to work in the Ministry of Health or to join the Medical College that had been established at King Saud University. Dr. Hussein Al-Gezairy had been appointed the Dean of the Medical College.

I asked for some time to think about this. I mulled over the two options for some time. Working in the university would keep me in direct contact with the academic life that I had grown to love so much. The salary and benefits at the university would be much higher than what I would get at the Ministry of Health. The salary was appealing especially because I was at the cusp of my career life. I now had a family to support, and every Riyal earned could help. On the other hand, I had spent almost my entire life in a classroom, studying. It was time to step into the real world and get involved. I yearned for this involvement, to put into practice all that I had learned and studied at university. In the end, my desire to show my mettle and change the existing healthcare system outweighed all other considerations. I prayed to Allah for guidance and I went to the Minister of Education and informed him of my decision: I wanted to work at the Ministry of Health.

There were two job openings at the Ministry of Health that matched my specialty. Both jobs were at level twelve of the old employment system. One was as the Director of Planning, Budgeting, and Programming Department. The other was the Director of Primary Healthcare. The Director-General of Preventive Medicine at the Ministry of Health, Dr. Hashim Al-Dabbagh, gave me the opportunity to choose whichever position I desired.

Although healthcare planning was my subspecialty for the Dr. PH degree I had obtained, planning was a very broad field with no boundaries. I believed that I did not have enough practical experience to head this department, so I decided to take the post of the Director of Primary Healthcare.

In my first week on the job at the Ministry of Health, we received a visit from Dr. Brown, an epidemiologist from the World Health Organization. I was assigned to accompany Dr. Brown on his trip to Jizan to study an epidemic that had spread there. I had never met anyone so eloquent and as powerful a speaker as Dr Brown. He could transition from story to story with ease; he could initiate a conversation and hold you enthralled by his words. He had such exceptional conversational skills that he led discussions, even when the Deputy Minister of Health, Dr. Hashim Abdul Ghaffar was present. Knowing Dr. Abdul Ghaffar, it was hardly likely that anyone other than he himself would lead a discussion if he was present.

During our two-week trip to the Southern region of the Kingdom, Dr Brown regaled me with interesting stories he told so amazingly well one after the other. I was so engrossed in a long story he was telling me about his travels in Indonesia that we actually missed our flight.

The purpose of our trip to Jizan was to investigate the alarming rate of increase in the spread of schistosoma after the Jizan Dam northeast of Abu Arish was built. Schistosoma, more commonly known as blood-flukes, are parasitic flatworms that are responsible for infections in humans. Infection caused by blood-flukes is considered by the World Health Organization as the second most devastating parasitic disease after malaria, with hundreds of millions infected worldwide.

After our study, we suggested a number of important solutions. The Department of Health implemented the measures we had proposed, and indeed there was regression in the spread of the disease.

Is it reasonable to say that we played a significant role in protecting hundreds of people from falling prey to this disease? Maybe, but the problem with working in preventive medicine is that its impact on the lives of people is not readily recognized. A high-tech, complicated surgery to remove a tumor or an enlarged spleen or to repair a defect in the heart, is celebrated in the media everywhere for days. The media will cover the story of a risky life-saving procedure and secure fame and glory for the surgeon, but the story of physicians who practice long-term preventive medicine and protect societies from infectious parasites such as blood-flukes hardly get a mention. No one hears or reads about these health workers, but Allah will give them ample rewards, by His will.

The schistosoma epidemic in Jizan is one illustration of the negative impact human beings have on the environment. Human behavior, such as dam building, changing the course of rivers, deforestation, and building of factories, have caused an imbalance in the delicate ecosystems of the Earth. In turn, diseases spread if we do not take the necessary precautionary measures to prevent them.

There are rivers in Europe that seem dead and lifeless. Polluted air and contaminants from factories have contributed to acid rain and other destructive agents that have flowed into these rivers and wiped out all life from them.

A study conducted in Egypt found that after the construction of the Aswan High Dam, the incidence of schistosoma infections multiplied in certain regions. The same problem occurred when Egypt's agricultural system was transformed from seasonal agriculture to crop irrigation. How true is the old saying, "Man is his own worst enemy."

Dr. Brown and I continued our travels. We flew to Najran to examine the healthcare services in the region. We also had the opportunity to visit the impressive archaeological and historical sites in Najran, including the ruins of Al-Ukhdud. How I wished we had made greater efforts to preserve and show off the rich history and past civilizations of these sites in the Arabian Peninsula!

When we were in Najran, Dr. Brown received a telegram from his wife in Geneva informing him that his son had been diagnosed with a terminal illness. She pleaded with him to come back as quickly as possible. I was right beside him when he read the telegram. He thought for a moment and then said, "What is can I do? We must complete our mission here first."

We successfully completed our mission.

Before we went our separate ways, Dr. Brown sensed the passion and fervor of youth in me. He said, "Dr. Sebai, I am confident that if you had been asked to pave a road, brick by brick, from Najran to Riyadh, you would have done it."

What he was hinting at was the fact that although it is a good thing to have high ideals and expectations of oneself, this can be catastrophic if there are no controls. Sometimes, placing demands on oneself beyond what is required and beyond one's capacity can be very exhausting.

We parted ways from Najran. Dr. Brown took a plane to Riyadh, and I rode a truck to Abha and from there to Taif. I wanted to explore regions of my country that I had never seen. I stopped in Abha, which back then was no more than a small village. It was so isolated that finding a restaurant was near impossible when the Director of the Department of Health Affairs, Dr. Abdul Lateef Kurdi, invited me to lunch.

I spent a few days in Abha, investigating the health status and health services there. I found that less than 1% of the children in the Asir region were vaccinated against childhood diseases. Today 90% of the children in the region receive immunizations. After my visit to Abha, I wrote my first report and submitted it to the Ministry of Health.

The findings of my brief study in Abha and my research in Turaba showed that infant mortality rate in rural areas of the Kingdom was 120 per 1,000. That meant that out of every 1,000 newborns, 120 died before reaching the age of one. Infant mortality rate today is 20 per 1,000. I estimated that if we were able to vaccinate 80% of the children in the Asir region, we could cut infant mortality rate in half. My proposal showed that this project would be cost-effective and could be implemented with clear planning, hard work, and a standard protocol. I wrote my suggestions in a report which I presented to the Ministry of Health, but for some reason that I never got to know, my proposal was never effected.

I traveled from Abha to Taif, riding in the open trunk of a truck. The truck driver sped through the desert and swerved around bends on hills on unpaved roads. He stopped for nothing except to refuel his truck and get some nourishment of tea and shisha. He proudly boasted that he was taking Congo pills (amphetamines), which helped him stay awake all day and night. I prayed to Allah to keep me safe from the dangers of amphetamines, stimulants, tranquilizers, and all drugs. By the grace of Allah, we arrived safely in Taif.

To my surprise, when I returned to Riyadh, I found that the Ford Foundation invited by the Saudi government to help reorganize the planning body and administrations of the ministries in the Kingdom had recommended that the young doctor who had graduated from the US with a Doctorate degree in international health should be appointed as the Director of Planning, Budgeting, and Programming Department. Overnight, I had become the Director of one of the major departments at the Ministry of Health. I must admit that at the time my knowledge of healthcare planning was limited to the knowledge I had acquired from books. I gained experience and more knowledge through my work at the ministry.

I can relate several stories about myself and my supervisor, the Health Deputy, Dr. Hashim Abdul-Ghaffar. We often had differences of opinion. These differences were to be expected between a young doctor, at the start of his career with some knowledge and very little experience and an older man at the helm of affairs at the ministry with immense responsibilities and the maturity and wisdom of his years. The older man was familiar with the politics within the ministry; he knew the rights and responsibilities of working in the ministry, unlike the young, energetic man who believed he could change the world.

On some occasions, when I disagreed with Dr. Abdul Ghaffar, I openly voiced my opinion to others. I ran into difficulties on several occasions because of my disagreements with Dr. Abdul Ghaffar. No doubt, everyone has the right to disagree with his supervisor. However, looking back, I realize that my thoughts and opinions on certain issues should have remained between myself and my supervisor. I should not have articulated these conflicts to other people. If I knew then what I know now, I would have been more circumspect and careful and a little more mature in my dealings with my supervisor. I would have gone directly to Dr. Abdul Ghaffar privately, and clearly and honestly explained my reasons for feeling so strongly about issues. I should have tried to convince him, but let him know that ultimately, he had the final say. However, how could a young, recently graduated doctor, full of fervor and energy of youth, have the maturity, the wisdom, and the calm of an older more experienced man?

I also want to add that despite our differences and disagreements, Dr. Abdul Ghaffar never did me any harm or threaten my position at the ministry, even though he had the power to do so. That is what true greatness is!.

A few months ago, I met Dr. Hashim Abdul Ghaffar at an event. He had retired from work at the ministry. We greeted one another with wide smiles and hugs and I said to him, "Dr. Hashim, you used to twist my ear when I worked with you at the ministry, but I declare that I learned so much from you and I owe you a lot."

As we were leaving the banquet hall, I noticed that I was ahead of Dr. Abdul Ghaffar, so I slowed down until he overtook me and as he came just in front of me, I said to him, "Dr. Hashim, the eye does not rise above the eyebrow."

Chapter 8

Riyadh University

I started work as an assistant professor in the College of Medicine in Riyadh University in the year 1973 (the name of the university was later changed to King Saud University). For seven years, I enjoyed working side by side with an exceptional group of colleagues. The College of Medicine was founded in four rented villas in 1969. Resources, human and financial, were limited. Despite that, the quality of education was of a reasonably high standard. Visiting professors from the United Kingdom and the United States attested to the university's high level of education. The teaching staff were no more than 30. Less than half of them were Saudi and the rest were of different nationalities. They laid a solid foundation, the very first blocks for the academic institution that has graduated over 2500 doctors: men and women.

The limited resources challenged our capabilities but motivated us to excel. The department of public health that I founded comprised the head of the department, one secretary and I. The head of the department, Dr. Ahmad Muhammad Sulaiman, also presided over the department of Forensic Medicine. For the first two years at the college, I only taught and did research. I spent my time with my students or at the library, but had no administrative responsibilities whatsoever.

The focus of my teaching was discussions. I would direct my students to the topics they needed to read before coming to class. In class, I opened the discussion on the topic using visual aids. My experience confirmed that this method of education was far more effective than lecturing. Knowledge was retained at a far higher rate, and classes were more enjoyable and interesting. This interactive learning requires much effort on the part of both the student and the teacher. The teacher must have a broad grasp of the subject and the student is expected to read the material before coming to class to be able to participate and add value to the in-class group discussion.

Skeptics may say that Arab students, in general, are not accustomed to this active type of learning, which demands reading before the class. Skeptics will say that students would rather rely on listening to the lecturer, take notes, and prepare themselves for exams.

However, from my own experience, once students as well as teachers become exposed and familiar with this type of active learning they enjoy it and take it on board. Students do in fact enjoy classes, and learn more effectively than when they sit in class and passively listen to the professor's lecture. Sometimes in the fall or spring we held the discussions outside in the garden. Today, when I meet students whom I once taught, they passionately recall how much they had benefited from our discussions.

I have a story to share with my readers that shows that when students read before class, raise questions, look for answers, and participate in discussions, they find classes far more interesting.

In one of my classes, I planned to cover the topic "tuberculosis". The question was that if there was plenty of information on tuberculosis in the library, why couldn't the students read selected literature on it and come to class to participate in a lively and intelligent discussion with their fellow students?

One week in advance, I announced to my students what the next topic of discussion was going to be. They were given a list of references to read. One of the students was to go the Tuberculosis hospital fetch a patient and come with him to class. (It takes prolonged exposure to a patient to contract the disease)

In class, the students curiously gathered around the tuberculosis patient inquiring about present complaint, past history, family history, housing conditions, eating patterns. They had already studied how to interview a Tb patient on their own. Some students examined the patient clinically. They then engaged in a long discussion about the patient: his diagnosis, treatment, prognosis and preventive measures for his contacts. My role was to facilitate the process of learning rather than feed them with knowledge.

After class, some students visited the hospital to collect further information on the subject and find out the extent to which Tb was a problem in the country. Another group of students visited the patient's home to meet his family members, get a first-hand view of his living environment, and discover if any member of the family had any symptom of the disease.

You may ask if the discussions were held in Arabic or English. Until very recently, I had accepted the norm that medicine must be taught in English. That is how our old professors had taught us and that is how my colleagues were teaching their students. All the while, I had this lingering feeling that this practice, which we had become so accustomed to, defied all common sense and logic. The Arabic language, the language of the Qur'an was in no way inadequate when it came to science and technology. It had been the language that illuminated the world a thousand years ago with discoveries in science, algebra, astronomy, medicine, and more. That was my believe in the early days in the College.

What increased my discontent with teaching medicine in English was what I saw of the students in my classes. Since the proficiency in English of the majority of the students was low, they were reluctant to participate in discussions. They only wanted to write down what the professors were saying in order to memorize their notes later for the exams. Many of them could neither read nor write English well; Their lack of competence in the language slowed them down. It interfered with learning. This language deficiency lasted, for many of them, until the final years of medical school. For those who did not study abroad, they continued to struggle with English long after graduation. Similarly, most of the Arab professors at the university spoke pidgin English, and they lectured in a mixture of Arabic and English.

I became more and more convinced that when one learnt in a language one was not proficient in, one would not reap the full benefits of what is read.

Later, I met Dr. Ahmad Sulaiman, the professor of Forensic Medicine, who was an avid proponent of teaching medicine in Arabic. According to him if we wanted to produce excellent doctors who would make breakthroughs in medicine and science, then we should teach them in their mother tongue. Nevertheless, a doctor has to master at least one foreign language.

This idea resonated with me. To make sure that there were indeed enough Arabic medical texts books, I wrote to the World Health Organization (WHO) and to some Syrian universities, which taught medicine in Arabic. They provided me with no less than 100 textbooks in Arabic covering all medical subjects which students needed for undergraduate study. Today, that number must have doubled. I conducted a study among a sample of students and lecturers, which became the basis of my book 'My Experience in Teaching Medicine in Arabic',

I return to the question, "In which language did I teach"? At the time, there were only English textbooks in the medical library. The students did their reading in English in preparation for discussions. In class, I reminded my students that I would speak Arabic and that they had the option to speak Arabic or English. Within minutes the students started to speak Arabic; expressing themselves and participating in discussions that became very lively and intriguing.

For those who argue that medicine should be taught in English, I say that the medical terms in the textbooks are quite small in number. Only 3% of the words used in a medical book (ignoring repetition of the same word) are medical terms. To illustrate this, please consider the following statement made by one doctor to another.

"I had a patient yesterday who complained of sore throat and fever. I conducted rigorous tests, including blood tests, throat swab and chest x-rays. I found all the results to be normal, except for leukocytosis (a high white blood cell count). My impression was that it was tonsillitis. The patient was given antibiotics and a special diet and plenty of rest recommended. I suggested that the patient visit an ENT specialist after he recovers to find out if surgery is necessary."

Out of approximately 80 words, only two were medical terms. The remaining words were every-day words that regular people use.

My argument in no way undermines the importance of learning English and the ability to read with ease and speak it fluently. It is extremely important for medical students to learn English or another foreign language, in order to continue their education and research and stay abreast of new developments in medicine.

Studying medicine in English does not necessarily improve the student's language skills. What is of more value and benefit to the student as a means of improving his or her English language skills is to actually focus on studying the language: its rules, grammar, syntax, and idiom. Regularly reading newspapers and magazines in English is an excellent way to practice the language. Industrialized nations such as Scandinavian countries, Holland, and Japan do just that. Students learn medicine in their own native language but are required to master a second language.

If it were up to me to make the decision, I would teach medicine in Arabic. However, no student would be eligible for graduation from medical school unless he/she obtained a high score in an English exam.

The World Health Organization also calls for reverting to the use of Arabic in medical schools in Arab countries. Likewise, the Ministers of both

Health and Education from all Arab countries convened several times under the umbrella of WHO and came out with the same recommendation: the language of instruction for medical education should be Arabic. Many medical professors agree that our universities should switch to the Arabic language. Students who participated in class discussions in Arabic showed a passion and interest for learning, which they lacked when they were struggling to understand and express themselves in English.

After this important consensus, the perplexing question still is. why has the change of medical education from English into Arabic not yet began? What are we waiting for? Why do we hesitate? I am not certain of the answer, but I imagine it is a difficult task that none is willing to initiate. It may also be the fear of the unknown.

In addition to the issue of the language, I was, and still am concerned about the conventional teaching methods which are common in most medical colleges. Throughout their studies and training, medical students are confined within the walls of a classroom and the hospital corridors. It would be more logical to take students for a while beyond these walls, and allow them to learn in a different environment, in the midst of people and society. Diseases do not come to people in the hospital but rather outside in the community. Patients who contract a contagious disease or have a chronic health problem do not get it in a lecture hall but rather outside in the society.

Our students should be out in the community, exploring the environmental factors, the social, economic, cultural factors that influence health and disease. Teaching students as they sit in a classroom only, or go around in the hospital, does not give young doctors the capability of meeting the health needs and demands of their society.

I proposed to the Faculty Board that we should incorporate community-based training in our curriculum. Students should mingle with people, live their everyday lives, survey people's health, and take a closer look at environmental conditions that may be affecting their health. My request was that we take the fourth year medical students, on field trips to villages to conduct health surveys and provide such health services as immunization, health education and nutritional programs.

A meeting was held by the Board to discuss this and take a decision, or more accurately put, to refuse my proposal. Some faculty members showed indifference to my ideas, and others expressed outright objection to such views. The overall sentiment was that "there is no time for such frivolities."

At the time, I was not a board member of the college of medicine, but I was invited by the dean to attend the meeting in order to explain the premise of my proposal. I understand now that anger is a destructive emotion when left unchecked, but on some occasions, anger can be the means of defending an idea and stand for what you believe in. And that is exactly what happened that day. I was so angry when I heard the decision of the board that I could not contain my emotions any longer. I exploded!

Overtaken by a passion for teaching and a desire to bring about change, I said, "I regret that I belong to a medical college that fails to see the importance of teaching students to find the root causes of disease, how the disease arises, develops, and progresses. Medical education should focus on teaching doctors to prevent disease before it impacts on society, rather than wait for the disease to take its hold on the patient making him so sick that he has to come to hospital to seek treatment for a disease that could have been prevented. My request should not be considered unusual. Many reputed universities around the world encourage their students to go out into the community to investigate the causes behind disease, and to learn methods of prevention."

It seems that my fervor and passion may have had an impact on some college board members, for they began to murmur and whisper to one another. Their minds were swayed and my proposal was approved, under two conditions: that our field work lasts no longer than one week, and the project be conducted at a minimal cost.

Our team consisted of 20 students and three professors. We traveled to Al-Madinah, and then to Taima, Al-Ola, and Madain Saleh. There we studied – the very basics of - malnutrition, malaria, and schistosoma (a parasite commonly known as blood-flukes). We examined patients and visited their homes. In the evenings, we discussed the health problems we had encountered and how they related to the peoples' lifestyle. We discussed how malaria and schistosoma were transmitted, and the social and environmental factors linked to their spread.

We collected data on childhood morbidity and mortality and measured heights and weights of a sample of children in the villages. We took blood samples for further investigations in our laboratories in the college. We immunized school children, and held health education awareness seminars for the mothers.

The students themselves organized all of these activities, and they did so with enthusiasm and a hunger to learn and serve. During their field work, the students applied first-hand some of what they had studied in their medical texts. They became aware of the role of environmental factors in the development of disease. They came close to the lives of ordinary people. They learned how some cultural and lifestyle practices can affect the health of the community.

Many of my previous students have become consultants, professors and deans of medical schools. When I occasionally meet them, we reminisce on those days spent in the field. Days that were vibrant with energy, self-reliance, hard work, compassion, and mutual affection.

After we returned from our field trip, the students talked about their experience and presented their activities and accomplishments to other people The people in authority in the University as well as my colleagues in the college seemed persuaded by the merits of our community approach. Apart from that, the students who participated in the field work obtained high grades in their community medicine examination.

In the following year, when I came to the faculty board to request for approval for a similar community exercise, consent was instant and unanimous. They not only approved, but welcomed my proposal. Professors from various departments of the college offered to accompany us on our trip.

It became a pattern for 4th year students of community medicine to participate in a two -week field trip every year. We visited villages in various parts of the country including Asir, Wadi Fatima, Qasim, Al-Majma'ah. We studied varieties of health problems such as leprosy, trachoma, road traffic accidents, traditional medicine and intestinal parasitic diseases and provided selected health services to the people of the community. Each year, we improved our technique and methods and we saw an increase in the budget allocated for our community activities and an increase in the number of staff members willing to participate in our field trips.

I would like to bring attention to the field trip we conducted in the year 1980. That was my last year at the medical college in Riyadh University, before leaving to Abha, to establish a medical college in there.

We selected Qasim, a region in the middle of Saudi Arabia to conduct our field work. It took us four months of traveling back and forth between Riyadh and Qasim almost every week to prepare for two weeks of field work. My colleague and I met with the Governor of the Region and other officials in the health, education and municipality sectors, to apprise them of the goals of our community work and the value of training our medical students at the community level. We had to select a village out of many villages in the Qasim

Region for our survey and training program. Among the most important criteria for the selection of our target village was that the villagers provide us with accommodation and transportation and participate in our activities. We wanted to develop a social network in the Region. When members of the community participate in our activities they were likely to feel a sense of belonging.

From the very beginning, we encouraged the students to take responsibility for organizing all activities and logistics of the field work. It was the students' duty to arrange our lodgings, meals, transportation, and purchases. We divided the students into committees, each with its share of responsibilities to be held accountable for how well they fulfilled their duties.

The day of our trip finally arrived. We drove from Riyadh to Qasim. We settled in one of the small villages in Al-Asyah District. Our group was around 50 made up of 30 medical students, 7 supervising professors, plus other helpers and volunteers from the village especially male and female school teachers.

There was much to gain and to learn from our trip to Qasim. All of us, students and professors lived a simple, non-frivolous life. We slept on mats on the floor, and ate whatever food was available. We interacted with villagers learning aspects of their values and traditions that have an influence on their health. Students gained a well-rounded knowledge about health and disease at the community level and how to work as a team. As for the professors, we conducted basic studies on some health problems, which appeared later on in a book.

Today, more than three decades later, I still remember vividly the series of field trips we conducted every year for five years in different regions of the Kingdom. I relive those amazing days that I spent with dear friends and colleagues who accompanied me on those trips: Siraj Malaika, professor of surgery, Ihsan Badr, consultant ophthalmologist, Siraj Zagzoug, professor of ENT, Hasan Abu Sabaa, internal medicine consultant, Abdul Rahman Al Suwailim pediatrics consultant, Faleh Al-Faleh, internal medicine professor, Mohsen Al-Hazmi, molecular medicine professor, Sameer Banoob, professor of international health and others.

Not every community health project met with flawless success. We ran into difficulties and obstacles, and we made mistakes. However, our driving force was to learn from our mistakes. In our first field trip, we did not systematically record and document our findings. At the end of the trip, we were unable to publish any of our findings. In our next field trip, we meticulously documented our data and published our findings. In our last trip to Qasim, we planned from the very beginning to write a book detailing our findings. The book was published by the Saudi Medical Journal, as a monograph, which became a reference text on the health status in a Saudi village.

The field work taught us the importance of engaging the community in healthcare activities. Before starting our activities, we would meet with community leaders to explain our purpose and the possible outcomes and the potential benefit of the community. We worked with school teachers in the villages to draw maps of the villages and numerate houses. We trained female teachers on how to operate film projectors in order to provide basic health education sessions to women. We were able to use the Health Centers of the villages for physical examinations and laboratory tests.

We learned the value of working together as a team, based on mutual respect and friendship. The conventional barriers between professors and students disappeared as we all worked together and had respect for one another.

We learned that all people had the potential for positive change and personal growth as long as they are given the opportunity. I remember, in one of our field trips, I asked one of my colleagues, Ihsan Badr, an ophthalmologist, to supervise a group of students in a field trip to Al-Majma'ah in order to study the prevalence of trachoma (a contagious viral infection of the eye). His immediate response was, "My focus will be on my own research. The students' role would be to help in collecting data."

Two years later, Dr. Badr had a shift in perspective. He joined us on our field trip to Qasim. I saw him moving around with his students, exchanging ideas with them, training them in the theory and practice of trachoma prevention.

I must admit a mistake common to most researchers that I made. In Qasim, I realized what our community work lacked only when we were almost at the end of the project. If I had been aware earlier in my life of this error, I would have corrected it from the beginning of my academic career.

Most, if not all researchers, conduct their studies with one goal in mind, which is: publication. Publication puts us in an esteemed position in academic circles. No doubt, scientists and researchers have noble goals of scientific discovery, discovery of the truth, finding a cure, and serving the community. However, there is an important goal that we tend to neglect, which is the application of the findings of our research to the real world. The recommendations that we usually write in the conclusion of our papers hardly ever find their way into action.

If you were to ask a researcher what he did with the results of his research and why he did not implement his recommendations, he would most probably reply, "My mission as a researcher is to investigate, document my findings, and publish the results. It is up to other people and organizations to implement them. "Who are those other people and organizations in our society?

In my opinion a researcher's mission should not end with the publication of his findings. This may be acceptable in the Western societies, where there are special organizations which implement the findings of research work. Billions of dollars are utilized in implementing the research findings, making new products, and putting them on the market for the public. Pharmaceutical companies spend huge amounts of money to translate academic research into products that can be sold. They gain enormous profits that far exceed what they spent to fund the research. Transforming theories into action is an industry.

I still remember, for example, when I was studying in Johns Hopkins School of Public Health that the Center for Disease Control (CDC) in Atlanta, Georgia, used to sponsor major research programs to be conducted by leading institutions such as Johns Hopkins University, George Washington University, and Emory University. The CDC spent millions of dollars on training doctors and healthcare workers to fight disease in society.

This is not the case in our societies. Such organizations do not exist. We cannot expect Ministries of Health in the Arab countries to take on this role as they have limited resources and are consumed by running public hospitals and healthcare centers.

A story from my personal experience comes to mind here. I told one of my superiors at the Ministry of Health about my DrPH dissertation that I had done and my research on the health status of the population in Turaba. He said to me, "Could you kindly give us a copy of your research paper so we can put it in the Ministry library." It is unfortunate that the fate of many of the research projects conducted in the Arab World is that they sit on library shelves, and are never used as a basis for the improvement of healthcare and implementation of disease prevention.

On another occasion, I was surprised when a certain department at the Ministry of Health asked me for the results of a study on leprosy I had conducted in the Kingdom. Although I had published the findings of this study ten years previously, no one had pursued the findings of this study or given its recommendations careful thought. Interest in this particular research had arisen only because the newly appointed Minister of Health demanded to see available statistics and research on leprosy in the Kingdom.

This problem exists not only in the Kingdom, but also in other developing countries and some international health organizations. A certain international organization assigned a research project to me, to study the human resources available in the healthcare system in Yemen. It took me a month to complete the research. A few years later, I met a researcher from the same organization conducting a study in Yemen on the exact same topic I had done earlier. I mentioned my study to him, but he told me that he had never come across it.

In our study in Qasim, we found that only a small number of children had been immunized. That was before the policy we take pride in today was drawn up, which demands that an immunization certificate of the newborn must be presented before the birth certificate is issued. We also found prevailing health problems among children such as intestinal parasites, respiratory infections, and trachoma, all of which are preventable diseases.

While in Qasim we designed a health promotion program that would involve the College of Medicine in Riyadh University, the Ministry of Health and the Ministry of Education as well as the community. Each had a role to play in a step-by-step plan. However, summer vacation started soon after we left Qasim,. After summer, I was assigned the responsibility of establishing a new college of medicine in Abha. Therefore, the comprehensive health promotion program we had painstakingly designed was consigned to the archives and remains unrealized.

I regret that during my academic career, I neglected to follow up the results of my research to make sure that they were implemented. If the results of my studies as well as other research results had been actually translated into an action, society would have benefitted a great deal. The fault lies first with researchers, but our establishments such as the Ministries of Health are also not without blame. Our academic institutions prepare us to test hypotheses, conduct research, analyze the data and publish. Our research mission ends with the publication of the findings, not with the application of the findings. There is also the problem of lack of communication and cooperation among universities and the governmental bodies and ministries that are ultimately responsible for protecting the people's health.

For example, over a period spanning two decades, eighty physicians specializing in family and community medicine have graduated from King Faisal University in Dammam. In order to obtain their fellowship degree they have to conduct a community -based research on a certain health topic. What has society gained from these studies? I have no answer. The response most probably is negative.

In the past two decades, I have examined and evaluated more than 15 medical research projects, sponsored by King AbdulAziz University of Science and Technology. The aim of the vast majority of the research was to shed light on certain health problems or assess the health status of a community. As I revised the research papers, I tried to draw attention to two issues. First, that society would benefit from the research if its findings and recommendations were actually implemented. Secondly, that the research papers should be published in Arabic.

In the Kingdom, a dozen medical journals have published more than 2000 medical papers over the last ten years. Almost all of the papers published are in English. If you were to ask why these papers were published in English, the authors would matter-of-factly state that scientific research must be published in English because it is the universal language for sharing knowledge. Researchers from anywhere in the world should be able to have access to our publications.

We must ask ourselves, where our priorities lie. What is our goal? Is it to make our research available to scientists across the world or to improve the health status of our society? It is more likely that the research will be better utilized and serve as a tool to make a positive impact on our society if it is published in Arabic. If there is a need to make our research accessible to scientists from other parts of the world, it would be easy to summarize the paper in English for distribution to every corner of the world.

Imagine someone working at the Ministry of Health trudging through the multitude of research on any given topic, to initiate a healthcare program in our community. Would he not learn more if the research paper was in a language that he could fully read, and comprehend? When he comes across a scientific paper in English, he will most probably, skim through it. Or he may even ignore it altogether, leave it on his desk, or put it away in the archives. Obviously, what I've stated refers to the majority, but not all of our administrators

Let us look beyond the boundaries of the Kingdom. In the Arab world, there are around 80 medical journals that have collectively published more than 20,000 medical articles in the last ten years. This truly is a treasure trove of knowledge which could have drastically improved the health status of our societies, had at least half of them been published in Arabic. This tremendous amount of research could be valuable resource for teaching medical students in Arabic, and used to improve the health status of our societies.

Interestingly enough, small countries such as Finland, Sweden, the Netherlands, and even Israel are known to teach medicine and publish many of their researches in their own languages. How wise is the famous great Muslim scholar, historian, mathematician, and philosopher, Ibn Khaldoon, who said, "The defeated admires the language of their conquerors."

The years that I worked at Riyadh University were rich with teaching and academic pursuits. I was not encumbered by administrative responsibilities. My only administrative position was as head of the department of community medicine. This freed me to get involved in what I truly loved: scientific research, field work, teaching, and service as a consultant for the World Health Organization, and prepare for the presentation of my weekly television program "Medicine and Life".

As a short term consultant to the World Health Organization, I was assigned several projects in Yemen, Oman, Iran, and Iraq.

My mission in Oman lasted one month. I studied the healthcare services in Oman and devised a plan to reform and improve the public healthcare system in the country. I visited Oman in the early years of the rule of Sultan Qaboos, after he took over reins of government from his father in a bloodless coup. Under his father's rule, Oman had been an underdeveloped isolated country, with its healthcare, education, and transportation systems lagging far behind its neighbors in the Gulf.

Qaboos modernized the country's economy, and undertook major educational reforms. He undertook a range of ambitious modernization projects, including construction of roads, hospitals, schools, communications systems, and industrial and port facilities. Gradually, Oman was linked to the outside world. A large number of Omanis, who had left the country under the previous regime, began to return to their rapidly developing country.

I clearly remember two incidents that demonstrate the progress made in the education in Oman. I drove to Muscat from the United Arab Emirates. I was stopped at the border because the visa which I had was for entering the country through the airport, not to come in through a land border. The border patrol needed to make a couple phone calls to the Ministry of Health and the Ministry of Foreign Affairs to get permission to allow me to enter. I noticed that the officers had been reading school books and preparing homework. While waiting for approval to let me through, I spent a couple hours helping them revise their lessons.

Another occasion was when we landed by helicopter on top of Al Jabal Al Akhdar (the green mountain) early one morning. As we walked to the healthcare center we had come to visit, I spotted a large crowd of students waiting outside their school. The gates of the school were still closed, but the students had their heads buried in their books, studying diligently. Curious, I asked, "Is it the week of final exams?" The answer I got was that it was not the exam week, but that this was a normal occurrence. Every-day, students arrived early, before the school doors opened, to revise their lessons and to get ready for classes. From that day, I predicted that the people of Oman would catch up with the rest of the world and quickly make up for the lost years. And indeed they have done so; the people of Oman have marked achievements in architecture, health services and education.

After my trip to Oman, WHO sent me on a mission to Yemen, to study human resources in the healthcare sector. I spent four weeks investigating the situation. Towards the end of my visit, I began to write my report, which the World Health Organization required me to complete before leaving Yemen. I looked for a quiet place to spend a few days to think clearly and write my report. I decided to go to Maarib. It was possible to kill two birds with one stone: finish writing my report there and visit Maarib Dam, one of the most amazing engineering marvels of the ancient world.

I flew on a small plane to Maarib. Upon the request of the government officials back in the capital, Sana'a, I was met by the sheikh of Maarib with a warm welcome. He took me to the only lodge in the small town, a mud-brick house, four stories high, on the top of a hill. It reminded me of the old houses in Makkah. The building was bare of any furniture except for a thin mat in a small room on the top floor. It was the only room that had an electric wire, which provided electricity to light up the room for a few hours at night.

My stay in this abandoned house lasted for three days and nights. I was the only guest there and I assumed that for a long time no one had lived there. The longest portion of my day was spent in writing. In the afternoons, I took walks on the outskirts of the valley until I reached the dam, where I stopped to take in the view and meditate on this marvel. On some occasions I was invited for a cup of tea. As soon as I heard the call to Maghreb prayer at the sunset, being a traveler, I combined both Maghreb and Isha prayers, and then returned to my deserted house enveloped in thick, quiet darkness.

I climbed to the bedroom on the top floor. The only electric light bulb in the whole house flickered and fretted to fight the darkness around it. Before long, the electricity went out, early in the first part of the night. I lay down on my back, staring up at the stars in the sky, until I finally drifted off to sleep.

What I dreaded the most during my stay there was the moment of stepping into the house in the darkness at night., It was pitch dark and I had to feel my way up the steps to the upper floor. All alone in the dark, I imagined all the creatures I had heard of in my early childhood: the genies, the ghosts, the evil spirits, and the monsters. I pray to Allah to forgive my aunts and other elderly women in our families, who filled our minds with frightening stories of the mysterious unseen world. The images that I pictured when I was a child came back to haunt me in that dark, isolated house in Maarib.

Early in the year 1973, events unfolded that changed life as we knew it, not only in Saudi Arabia, but most of the Arab world. Our brethren in Egypt gained victory over Israel. They were the first Arab nation to stand up against Israel and to show the world that Israel was not invincible. On October 6, 1973, Egyptian troops took Israel by surprise and crossed the Suez Canal. They seized the Bar-Lev Line of Israeli fortifications with the intention of pushing the Israelis out of the Sinai Peninsula. Simultaneously, Syria attacked the Golan Heights.

Six days after Egypt and Syria launched this surprise military attack against Israel, the US supplied Israel with arms. In response to this, Saudi Arabia and other oil exporting countries in the Gulf announced an oil embargo against Canada, Japan, the Netherlands, the United Kingdom and the US. OPEC (Organization of Petroleum Exporting Countries) members agreed to use their leverage over the world price-setting mechanism for oil to stabilize their incomes by raising world oil prices. Thus, market prices rose from $3 per barrel to $12 per barrel.

Saudi Arabia was the largest oil exporter, and the success of the embargo demonstrated Saudi Arabia's diplomatic and economic power. The sweeping economic boom that the Kingdom experienced resulted in widespread social changes as well. Overnight, it had become a rich country and had entered the race for development.

An article in the Time Magazine indicated that the Gulf countries in 1973 were at the threshold of transformation, that was nothing like any time period the area had witnessed since the Crusades. In an interview conducted by an American magazine, the president of one of the ministries in the Gulf region stated that he had in his possession millions of dollars for the government to spend, but he had not yet decided how and in which area it should be spent.

The Saudi Riyal increased in value. Investing in lands and real estate became the trend for everyone. A friend of mine who had been a professor at the university, told me several years later when the frenzy had quieted down in the 1990s, "I predicted at the beginning of the economic boom that this would be a once in a lifetime event, which would not repeat itself. I would either ride the wave or let it pass me by and leave me stranded on the shore. I refused the administrative position offered to me at the university and put my academic research on hold. I spent all my time in real estate offices, buying and selling lands and properties. I taught myself the trade. In less than a decade, by the end of the 1970s, I had made myself a fortune. I had become a multi-millionaire."

No doubt, my generation reaped the benefits of the rising global oil prices and the economic growth that resulted. Architectural, educational, and healthcare projects sprung up all over the country. We built universities and hospitals, paved roads and bridges, and connected electricity and phone lines to almost every home. Schools were built and we brought education to every city, town, and village in the Kingdom. However, because the development was so sudden and rushed, we were not adequately prepared, and today we are discovering some faults and deficiencies in the infrastructure of the country. I wonder if we would have learnt from our past mistakes had we entered another era of economic growth? Or is it simply human nature to forget the lessons learned of the past?

No doubt, the economic development contributed to the improvement of healthcare in the Kingdom. The average family gained many health benefits, not only as a result of the expansion of the healthcare system but also because of the rise in people's level of education, health awareness, and standard of living. We were able to reduce the prevalence of malnutrition, parasitic infections, and other childhood infectious diseases. It appears the economic boom was a double -edged sword, when it came to health. Although we controlled many infectious diseases, new degenerative diseases which had not been present in the country before began to manifest in greater numbers. The problems of heart disease, road traffic accidents, and stress- related disorders spiked in the post-oil embargo era. That is the price we had to pay for urbanization and change to city life. It is with romantic nostalgia that many of us long for those early, simple days.

In 1975, the assassination of King Faisal, may Allah have mercy on him, shook the country. It was a horrendous crime; a tragic event in Saudi history, and all people mourned his death.

While working as assistant professor in the university in Riyadh, I participated in many international health and medical conferences. I was invited as a guest speaker and a visiting professor to universities in Iraq, Libya, and Sudan. At the beginning of the year 1980, I was promoted to the position of professor at the university. One morning, I was called to the office of the Minister of Higher Education, Shaikh Hasan Al al-Shaikh. He gave me the responsibility to establish a college of medicine in Abha. From that moment, I knew that a challenging task lay ahead of me.

Chapter 9

Establishing the College of Medicine in Abha

The decision was made to establish the College of Medicine in Abha, under the direct control of the Minister of Higher Education. The Minister put me in charge and appointed me the dean. He gave me the latitude to request for whatever I needed to lay the foundations of the college, be they financial, administrative or academic. In this early phase, I needed to be able to proceed and work with as few limitations and bureaucratic routine as possible. At the same time, I understood that with these great privileges came grave responsibilities.

I traveled to Abha; and my initial step was to choose the location for the College of Medicine. When I first arrived in Abha, I was greeted by Abdullah Abu Milha, one of the highly respected leaders in the town, from a noble family with a long history in Abha. He spent several days introducing me to government officials and helped to arrange interviews with important policy-makers. I met with the Governor of Abha, His Royal Highness King Khalid Al-Faisal, who was a gifted poet and a brilliant leader and administrator. I also met the Vice-Governor of Abha, His Royal Highness Prince Faisal bin Bandar, the current Governor of Riyadh region. They both put at my disposal a wide range of resources I would need to ensure the success of the establishment of the College of Medicine.

To begin my plans for laying the foundations of our college, I made an extensive tour of some of the best medical colleges in Europe, the United States and Canada. I visited and explored the universities that had adopted an innovative approach to teaching, which was heavily reliant on self-learning, community-based and integrated approach. This new approach immerses the students in the social environment and incorporates the health problems and needs of their society in its syllabus.

I visited prestigious universities such as Newcastle Medical School in the United Kingdom, McMaster University Medical School in Canada, Maastricht University in the Netherlands, and Stanford University in the United States. On my return trip, I stopped in Geneva to visit the World Health Organization to broach the idea of the new medical school.

The aim was to establish a medical school that would prepare doctors to provide holistic healthcare; doctors who were capable of preventing and treating disease, and improving the health status of the society. We wanted doctors who would treat the person not the disease. We needed doctors who would perceive their patients not as cases, but as humans with body, mind, and soul. Our prospective medical students should be able to excel in independent learning and continue their education, conduct basic scientific research, and train and teach others. To be able to achieve such high expectations and lofty goals, we needed a well-planned strategy that would get the cooperation of all branches of government and community, and also learn from the experiences and successes of international medical universities.

We held a number of conferences in which professors and deans from different medical schools and universities, both local and international participated. We wanted to make use of the expertise of the best medical schools to define the goals, design the framework for the curriculum and learning practices for each year of the medical school. This process took about six months.

It would have been possible to save ourselves a great deal of work by simply choosing a curriculum from an existing medical school in the West or in the Arab world, and making a few changes for use in the College of Medicine in Abha. However, from the very beginning, we understood that our painstaking way of designing the curriculum was the best if we wanted to establish a unique medical school. There is no one-size fits all when it comes to medical education.

Our philosophy from the inception of the College of Medicine was one of cooperation between all departments of the college; They were to complement and support each other, rather than compete with one another. In addition, we intended to remove the barriers between the student and the professor, and between the student and the society. The curriculum of the college would require medical students to get involved in society, conduct studies, and collect information on the health problems, including the causative factors of disease in the society. Medical students should be trained in disease cure and prevention, while they learn by means of scientific discourse, research, in addition to the lectures they attend.

Whenever we received visiting professors or visiting deans of a College of Medicine from a foreign university, we took them on a tour of the beautiful region in the helicopter which the Governor of Abha kindly provided. We showed them the tops of the towering mountains of the Asir region and we took them to the villages, the markets, and the healthcare centers, and also arranged a meeting with the local people of the region. We wanted our consultants to see and have a feel of the environment and society in which our medical school was going to be built. Our medical school in Abha was to be established to the highest possible scientific standards to meet the present and future needs of our people in the cities, villages and the nomadic Bedouins.

Our guests were mesmerized by the beauty of Asir, its majestic mountains, green fields, seemingly bottomless valleys, and the houses and villages scattered on the mountain tops. I remember, one visiting professor telling me that he had never ever seen such natural beauty and magnificence in all of his travels

I was certain that the best method for instruction in medicine was a multi-faceted approach. I strongly believed that students learnt more effectively when they searched for information, conducted research and surveys, participated in discussion, expressed their views and listened to the contrary opinions. Students need to occasionally leave the classroom and step out into society where they can learn about the diseases and health needs of the community.

This innovative approach to learning first came into being in the 1950s, in some medical schools in the North America, and gradually spread to medical schools in the Europe and Australia. It was a slow start, because it challenged the traditional method of teaching in universities where students sat in class and listened to the professors' well-orchestrated lectures. In a few short years, the number of universities that had adopted this novel approach to learning had multiplied. The results of this new method of learning that had replaced the older, traditional, conventional one were astoundingly positive.

This innovative approach had not yet found a place in our Region. Would our professors and students be receptive to this novel approach? Do we have the resources necessary to ensure the success of this method? Is it suitable for the culture and educational environment in the Kingdom? These questions swirled around in my head. My colleagues who would be the faculty for the future medical school shared my concerns as we set out to design the curriculum. Collectively, we reached the conclusion that the innovative approach was not only possible in our country, but it was highly desirable.

We recommended the innovative approach as the methodology of instruction for the College of Medicine, while keeping in mind the following three issues:

1. It is not in the best interest of the new College of Medicine or its students to simply borrow the curriculum from an existing medical school. A curriculum should be tailor-made to fit the environment, culture, and resources available in our society.

2. Skills development and training courses must commence immediately for the faculty of the College of Medicine. Greater effort, experience, and skill are required of the professor using the innovative approach to teach than is necessary for a professor to prepare the traditional lecture and presentation. In the past, some professors may have used the same lecture notes and slides year after year. The method of instruction we aspired to use at the medical school in Abha, would require the professor to guide and prompt students to search certain sources for information and learn. The student would then come to class with a solid background of knowledge to discuss, hypothesize, debate, and apply what he has learned.

3. Flexibility is a necessity, especially in the initial phases of our project. Unanticipated problems may arise which would require quick decision making, flexibility, and the willingness to adapt to change, for rigidity is an obstacle to growth and development.

When we adopted the innovative approach to teaching at the College of Medicine in Abha, there were only 80 other universities worldwide that had successfully implemented this ingenious approach. Today, over thirty years later, we find a couple hundred medical schools in different parts of the world using the innovative approach with some variations, but all with the same goal: that of training doctors for a lifelong process of continued self-learning and research; producing doctors who are as adept and knowledgeable in disease prevention as they are in treatment.

What was the response to this? How did the society react to the use of this innovative approach at the newly established medical school in the university of the small, humble town of Abha? At the time, there were 30 medical schools in the Arab world, only two of which like us were beginning to implement the innovative approach in learning: the University of Gezira in Sudan and Suisse Canal College of Medicine in Egypt. The Arab Gulf University at Bahrain was still in the planning phase and its mission and curriculum were still unclear.

Today, as I write my memoirs, thirty years after the College of Medicine in the university in Abha was founded, the innovative approach is the leading method of teaching in universities around the world. Hundreds of medical schools have adopted this approach in recent years.

While we laid the initial building blocks of the medical school in Abha, there were those who supported our view, and they were a minority; and there were those who were opposed our viewpoint, and they made up the majority. Another group remained neutral.

Those who were opposed to our position claimed that it would be unwise to use a new approach to teach in a new medical college in the Kingdom, until it had been successfully tried elsewhere with proven results. In reality, the creative and innovate method of teaching was not new or unfamiliar to Islamic culture; its roots are to be found in the traditional method of teaching throughout the history of the Muslim civilization. A short probe into history and medical classes would reveal that such methods were used by such great doctors as Al-Razi, Avicenna and Al-Zahrawi, at a time when the sciences, mathematics, and medicine flourished in the Islamic world. Teaching during that era of enlightenment that illuminated the whole world, depended on discussion, debate, self-study, and a search for answers.

There was another obstacle. Initially, we had estimated that it would take two years of planning to set up the College of Medicine at Abha. By the end of our first year, major administrative changes had taken place. The college that was initially directly under the jurisdiction of the Minister of Higher Education was brought under the umbrella of Riyadh University (currently King Saud University). Our innovative method of teaching met with stronger opposition from the administration of the university in Riyadh. It became clear that we would not be able to implement the new approach for the College of Medicine in Abha for which I had great hopes. I felt compelled to return to the academic world, and distance myself from the administration and politics of running a medical school. I longed to resume my research, to study, and to teach; but most of all I felt I needed a year off to dedicate myself to research.

I received two offers: one was to establish a College of Medicine at the Arab Gulf University in Bahrain, and the other was to create a Master's degree program in Family and Community Medicine at the Armed Forces Hospital in Riyadh. I chose the latter because I felt that it was an excellent opportunity to develop a strong foundation for future higher education in the field of public health.

After I left the university in Abha, the position of the dean of the College of Medicine was filled by Dr. Ghazi Jamjoom, a prominent professor in virology. I am very happy to say that the College of Medicine moved in the right direction during his tenure and that of the dean who succeeded him. The college flourished and achieved most impressive results. Over 1,000 well trained doctors have so far graduated from the College of Medicine in Abha. Its approach to teaching was that of a middle ground between the creative, innovative and the more traditional approach. The commencement ceremony for the first class of graduates of the College of Medicine, in the presence of the Governor of the region was a stupendous event. Having laid the foundation stones for the College of Medicine, I was overwhelmed with joy and a feeling of tremendous accomplishment.

Chapter 10

King Faisal University

Before receiving the offer from the Armed Forces Hospital to establish a higher education program in public health, I had made plans to take a sabbatical year to dedicate my time to research, writing and publication. I had decided to spend the sabbatical year at the College of Medicine at the University of San Diego in the United States. My choice of this particular university was influenced by professor, Dr. Hanlon, a faculty member of the College of Medicine at the university. I admired his work and had read his books while studying for my Master's and Doctorate degrees.

All travel preparations had been completed and I was ready to leave, but there was still some sense of uncertainty and misgivings., I had a family, and my children were in school. Just then I received the offer from my friend, Dr. Abdul Hameed Al-Faraidi, the Deputy Director of healthcare services at the Armed Forces Hospitals (MODA) for the position of the Dean of postgraduate medical study. I accepted that offer and decided to remain in the Kingdom.

I spent two years establishing a fellowship program in public health at the Armed Forces Hospital. These two years were immensely productive and rich in personal growth. With fewer administrative duties, I had time to focus on the work at hand: laying a foundation for the program of higher medical education. I even had time to do some research, reading, and writing. During this period, I was able to complete two books; "the Health of the Family in a Bedouin Community" published in English and Arabic and "Health in Saudi Arabia Vol. I ". In addition, I had several medical articles published on the epidemiology of diseases in the Kingdom.

This was the beginning of the economic boom in the Kingdom. Our hopes, ambitions, and dreams were larger than our capabilities of implementing the programs and projects we aspired to. With the growth in the economy, MODA appointed a private company to do a feasibility study to establish a postgraduate program in family and community medicine. As part of the study, the company organized a medical conference in Italy. Participants were invited from North America and Europe to discuss the Saudi program. The conference was held in a breathtaking resort on Lake Como, one of the most beautiful resorts in Italy. I was curious as to reason for the choice of such a venue, an exotic and expensive resort in Europe for the medical conference on Saudi Arabia rather than in the Kingdom.

On the first day of the conference I raised the issue "Why are we holding the conference, which is supposed to discuss a Saudi project in Italy rather than in the Kingdom?"

The reply was that, "If we held the conference in the Kingdom, hardly anyone would attend."

To me that answer was unacceptable, so. I directed my question to the audience. "If you were invited to participate in this meeting in Saudi Arabia would you attend?" Hands went up across the meeting hall.

Eventually, what was going on behind the scenes became clear to me. The company wanted a piece of the pie; everyone wanted to claim their share of the so called windfall in our country. Its contract with MODA was based on "cost plus". It asked for an exorbitant sum of money to implement the program. Their proposal included an annual salary in excess of SR one million for the director of the proposed program. This did, not include other benefits. As was to be expected the proposed program was rejected.

In the two years that I worked at MODA, I signed an agreement with King Faisal University to redesign the MODA Program of Family and Community Medicine for the university. I realized that it was the right time for me to step away from governmental posts, gain some independence and start my own company for health planning and programming. I established a private consultancy firm and attracted some young enthusiastic people to work with me. This gave me time to do some writing, and was able to complete "Health in Saudi Arabia- Vol. II" which was published in English and then translated into Arabic, and a book on "Health problems during the Hajj season". In addition, I continued to present my television program 'Medicine and Life'.

Although I was extremely busy, there was an incessant yearning for the academic life of the university I had left. The Family and Community Medicine program that I had been involved in establishing at King Faisal University was up and running. When I received an invitation from Professor Muhammad Saeed Qahtani, President of King Faisal University in the Eastern Province, to join the University there was no hesitation on my part.

It was not an easy move from Riyadh to Al-Khobar in the Eastern Province, especially for my family. My wife was teaching at a school for children with special needs in Riyadh. My oldest daughter was studying medicine at King Saud University, my son was still in the high school and our youngest daughter was in the kindergarten.. After much thought, we decided that my family would remain in Riyadh while I moved to the Eastern Province alone. I would make the journey of about a three and a half hour drive between Riyadh and Al-Khobar every weekend to visit my family.

I became a staff member of the Family and Community Medicine Department at King Faisal University Medical College. I joined an amazing group of colleagues from different parts of the world: Egypt, Sudan, India, Australia, and New Zealand. I was the only Saudi professor. That was back in 1986. Today, Saudis make up the majority of staff in universities.

We came from different roots and cultures, but we shared one goal: to lay a strong foundation for a postgraduate program in Family and Community Medicine. The first of its kind not only in Saudi Arabia but also in the Arab World.. I was witness to the devotion of the faculty members to their work. Likewise, the medical students who were accepted into the program were hard working and understood the great responsibility they were carrying, to serve the people. We were like a family; professors and students. I remember introducing my students as my family at a meeting with the Minister of Health Faisal Al-Hejailan,.

The King Faisal fellowship program in Family and Community Medicine that we established at the university takes four years to complete. The students were doctors who had chosen the practice of comprehensive health care as their career. Together with their lectures, seminars, group discussions, and clinical training in hospitals and health centers, a relationship with the society had to be forged. They were required to conduct community- based research of almost eight months as part of their program. Upon successful completion of the program, they would obtain the Fellowship of Family and Community Medicine. They could then become staff at the university or consultants of Family and Community Medicine in the health care system.

In the early 1970s, the Arab Ministers of Health had a meeting to discuss why they should still be dependent on western countries for the postgraduate training of their doctors. Why could they not provide postgraduate medical education to their doctors in Arab countries? It was possible, but it was a vision and a long term goal for the future. All that was required for this vision to be realized was the cooperation and collective efforts of the medical and academic institutions within the Arab world. From this initial idea, the Arab Board of Medical Specialties was born. Among those Ministers of Health at the time were: Dr. Abdul Rahman Al-Awadi, from Kuwait, Dr. Hussein Al-Gezairy from Saudi Arabia, Dr. Ali Fakhro from Bahrain and Dr. Iyad Al-Shatti from Syria. The names of these men will be remembered as pioneers of medical education in the Arab world.

The Headquarters for the Arab Board of Health Specialties was established in Damascus. The late Dr. Omar Bilail from Sudan was appointed the first President of the Board. Throughout my work with the newly established board, I realized that what bound us together as Arabs; the culture, language, and religion, were greater than the current politics that divided us. The harmony, cooperation, and support that we displayed within the Arab Board of Health Specialties was in fact a living example of what Arabs could achieve if they worked together as one nation and abandoned the petty squabbles with one another.

A European can work, buy a house, and own a business or company in any European countries he desires. He can travel from one European country to another with no restrictions of entry or exit visas. European countries have achieved this unity despite their differences in language, culture, and faith, and despite the old tensions and animosities of the past. Can we, in the Arab world, not do the same or even better?

Being a part of the Arab Board of Medical Specialties had been a wonderful experience. Those men, dedicated to the health and wellbeing of their communities, planted seeds for the development of healthcare in the Arab world. Five decades later, we harvest the fruits of what they sowed. Under the umbrella of the first Arab Board in Syria and other Medical Boards that followed in various Arab countries, thousands of doctors obtained postgraduate training and education in over 25 different medical specialties and sub-specialties and went on to serve their communities and countries.

At its inception, the Arab Board had four specialties; medicine, surgery, obstetrics and gynecology, and pediatrics. A few years later, a fifth specialty was created: family and community medicine. The new board made up of thirty members representing 15 Arab countries were university professors and deans of medical colleges, and government officials of Health,. I was nominated the president of the new Board. Several committees were created in order to design the curriculum, establish a bank of examinations, locate resources, and evaluate hospitals and primary health care centers for training.

We held our quarterly meetings in a different country each time. Naturally, we had our own differences of opinions and visions. As we worked together as a team, all of our political or national differences were erased. We had only one goal: that of training doctors to specialize in Family and Community Medicine. To give these doctors the knowledge and skills necessary to contribute to the development of health in the Arab world.

My position as president of the Arab Board of Family and Community Medicine lasted six years. I stepped down when I was appointed to the Shoura Council of the Kingdom. It would have been impossible to function in both positions at the same time.

I would like to touch on some of the important issues that occupied a great deal of my time and energy while working at King Faisal University in the Eastern Province. One important issue was the switch to the teaching of Family and Community Medicine in the Arabic language. Some of my colleagues and I had been contemplating this issue for some time. Our students in the department of Family and Community Medicine (FAMCO) spent around eight months conducting surveys, collecting data, analyzing results, and finally writing their thesis in order to obtain the fellowship in Family and Community Medicine.

The society they collected information from was Arab. The surveys were conducted in Arabic. The professors were mostly Arabs. The government officials in the Ministry of Health, who would implement the recommendations from these field work were Arab. What then was the benefit of writing the fellowship thesis in the English? Is the Arabic language deficient in communicating health problems and scientific findings, or are the shortcomings from us? We believed or rather some of us believed that writing the thesis in Arabic would be more appropriate. The believers were committed to pushing for the change.

We presented our idea to the departmental board. We did not face much opposition. If any members of the Board were opposed to the idea they did not show it. I assume they feared being labeled as imitators of the West or branded as disloyal to their heritage and their culture.

The next step was to present our proposal to the board of the college of medicine at King Faisal University. We argued that the university had stipulated as a general rule that instruction was to be in the Arabic language, unless it became a hindrance or became extremely difficult. We claimed that there should be no obstacle in the way of providing a solid medical education in Arabic. In fact, instruction in Arabic would enhance medical education in our country rather than impede it. We could benefit from the experiences of other successful medical colleges in countries such as Sweden, Netherlands, and Greece. In those countries, instruction in medical colleges was in their mother tongue, and their medical research and publications were written in their own languages. Why could our students of Family and Community Medicine not write their theses in Arabic?

The response from the board of the college of medicine was positive, especially after we stipulated that any student who chose to write his theses in Arabic had to write a detailed summary in English. One further step was to be taken and that was to get the approval of the University Board. Our initiative successfully passed. We were ecstatic. For the first time, it became acceptable to present scientific research in the field of medicine in the Arabic language in our part of the world. Syria served as precedent for us.

As some of our postgraduate students opted to prepare their research proposals in Arabic, some professors who opposed the idea started to spread rumors that this was unheard of and that it was inappropriate for the theses to be written in Arabic.

One student came to me, expressing his desire to write his thesis in Arabic. However, his external examiner was to be Dr. David Morley from the UK, and he did not know how to overcome the problem of presenting his thesis in Arabic to a Non-Arabic speaking examiner. I knew David very well. He is an amazing community medicine oriented pediatrician and researcher, who was awarded King Faisal International Prize as a pioneer in medicine for his achievements in improving children's health in Africa. He would be happy to examine a student who has written his thesis in his own mother tongue and provided an English summary. In the evening, I called David at home and explained the situation to him. He did not fail me and expressed his interest. I shared the David response with the student, but the negative remarks he had been hearing had a greater influence on him. He reversed his decision.

Another student, Mahdi Qadi, approached me. He decided to write his thesis in Arabic. We appointed Dr. Mohammad Shebrawi, an Egyptian

Professor as his external examiner. The day for the defence of his thesis finally came. The oral examination lasted two hours. The examiner, Dr. Shebrawi, announced, "I never imagined that I would evaluate a Fellowship thesis in Arabic, and here I am discussing Dr. Qadi's thesis in Arabic, which I grade as excellent!" This opened the door. Many other students followed suit; they presented their theses for the fellowship in Family and Community Medicine in Arabic.

Many stories could be told about the time I spent in King Faisal University and the close relationship I had with my students. On one occasion, I planned to attend a medical conference in Finland. Some of my students heard about this and asked if they could go with me to Finland. I gladly welcomed the idea and I suggested that after attending the conference we could study the primary healthcare system in Finland. We contacted the World Health Organization which helped by arranging with the Ministry of Health in Finland a study tour for our group to explore the health care system in Finland. The students were Nabil Qurashi, Saleem bin Mahfoudh, Sameer Sabban, and Muhammad Al-Ghamdi. They are now consultants and university professors. Today, whenever our paths cross we fondly reminisce about those unforgettable days we spent together in Finland.

It was their first time in Europe for my companions. Hotel expenses were higher than they had anticipated. I suggested that we move out of the hotel to a camping ground which would be lovely and far less costly. Camping grounds offer breathtaking views of nature, in the middle of a forest or by a river or a lake; it is a peaceful relaxing environment.

We spent a week camping on the outskirts of Helsinki. At the crack of dawn, we would leave the camp with our guide who had been assigned to us by the Finish Ministry of Health to visit hospitals and healthcare centers. After a long day of visits and meetings, we would return to the camp before sunset. A week passed with a treasure of knowledge of the health care system in Finland and enjoyment. We enjoyed the beauty of the camp area on the shores of a lake. We cooked our favorite traditional foods. It was a unique experience. We brought back and shared our experiences with our colleagues in Khobar.

In the following year, we traveled to Malaysia where we attended a medical conference and explored the healthcare system. The arrangements had been facilitated by the World Health Organization and the Malaysian Ministry of Health.

The plan was to continue these educational experiences as part of the international health course I was teaching. However, my move to the Shoura Council, put an end to those proposed annual trips.

Coming back to the health care system in Finland, which is in itself a lesson that many developing countries can learn from. It was an outstanding example of a regionalized health services system planned and implemented with the full collaboration of the people. As we all know, the health status of a society is determined by a number of factors such as the economic status, level of education, healthcare services and the environmental conditions. In Finland, all of these factors come into play, making it one of the top countries in terms of the health status of its people.

Healthcare in Finland is characterized by two important features: It is not centralized and members of the community play an active role in planning, implementation and follow up and evaluation of their health programs. The Ministry of Health in Helsinki has no more than 100 employees, mostly planners, programmers and evaluators. The responsibility of the Ministry is to devise policies related to healthcare and follow up and evaluate the results of the health service implemented by the local authorities.

The country is divided into regions. Each region is made up of municipalities (communes). The commune is inhabited by 10,000 to 100,000 people. Each commune is allocated a budget for its healthcare services. How this budget is spent is decided by a team of healthcare employees and volunteers from the community such as lawyers, engineers and businessmen. They have the full authority to plan and implement whatever health programs they deem suitable and necessary for their community as long as they fit into the general framework laid down by the Ministry of Health in Helsinki.

For example, supposing the Ministry of Health institutes a policy that infant death should not exceed 5 per 1,000 per year. It is up to the healthcare administration of each commune to implement their own programs to keep down the rates of infant mortality. Each commune can initiate different programs; a commune may establish a wellness center, or build a new department in the hospital, or create home care, or implement women and children health awareness or an education program for the commune. If a health project was too large and costly for one commune such as the building of a new hospital, it can collaborate with another to implement the project,

I dream of the day when healthcare authority in every region in the Kingdom has enough autonomy and leverage to plan, design, and implement its own healthcare programs within the general frame work laid by the Ministry of Health. I dream of seeing members of the society actively involved in planning and implementing health care programs in their communities.

My work at King Faisal University lasted eight years. Eight years filled with blessings, learning, and productivity. Khobar is a charming, unforgettable city, with clean streets, a peaceful atmosphere, and beautiful views of the sea. As I was freed of the managerial and administrative burdens, I wrote four books and published several articles in medical journals. With my colleagues, we founded the Arab Board of Community Medicine, the Saudi Society of Family and Community Medicine and the Saudi Journal of Family and Community Medicine. I continued to present my television program, Medicine and Life. In the mean time I had the opportunity to participate in humanitarian activities with the International Islamic Relieve (IIR) organization. Through IIR, I was sent on missions to promote health in Pakistan, Somalia, Bangladesh, the Philippines, and Albania. I feel I received more than what I gave; I gained experience in life, I explored different cultures, and related to diverse peoples of the world.

Over time, the importance of public health and preventive medicine became more evident and appreciated. When I graduated with the degree in public health (community medicine) and returned to the Kingdom in the year 1969, there were only three Saudi doctors in the Kingdom who were specialized in this field. Now, in 2016, there are over 400 doctors specialized in family and community medicine.

In order to initiate and implement public health activities in the society, our department founded the Saudi Society of Family and Community Medicine. I was elected the chairman. His Royal Highness, Prince Talal bin Abdul Aziz, was chosen as the Honorary President of the Society.

Soon, the Society had a branch in almost every one of the 13 regions of the country. Each branch was autonomous and had its own set of activities. Today, the Saudi Society of Family and Community Medicine is one of the most widespread and active health organizations in the Kingdom. One of its most significant accomplishments was the launching of the Saudi Journal of Family and Community Medicine, published in both Arabic and English.

A couple of my colleagues and postgraduate students undertook the translation of a book on International Health from English to Arabic. It was an educational and exciting experience mainly for our students. Translating a book is as important and challenging a task as writing one. Translating from one language to another is a science as well as an art. A word-for-word translation may lose the meaning and convey the wrong message. Besides, the translator runs the risk of omitting something vital in a translation based on the meaning,. Striking a happy medium in which the actual meaning of the text is retained, and smooth writing style maintained is indeed a challenge. Much practice is required for the acquisition of this skill. That was one of the main objectives of involving our students in the translation of the book.

Another of my experiences reflects a problem in the basic education system in the Arab World. I invited a number of medical professors from different Arab countries to contribute to a book about community medicine in the Arab language. To my surprise, many of the professors lacked the ability to articulate and write well in Arabic. Our basic education is to be blamed. Schools are quite ineffective and lacking in teaching the Arabic language.

One of the books that I wrote brought a wave of mixed responses from both the general public and the professionals. It was *"My Experience in Teaching Medicine in the Arabic Language. "*. The idea of the book came from a lecture I gave in the Cultural Club in Dammam. In my lecture, I explored the factors which had led to the teaching of medicine in the Arab world in foreign languages. Medical students receive their education in French in Morocco, Italian in Libya, and English in the remaining Arab countries with one exception, Syria, which teaches medicine in Arabic. The dominant reason behind this is the European colonization of Arab countries, which imposed their language, culture, and ideas on the colonized people. The influence of colonization became so deeply ingrained that we began to think that the colonizer's language was superior to our own, that theirs was the language of literature and science.

The great historian, Ibn Khaldoon, stated that whenever a society is conquered, the society gradually becomes assimilated into the conqueror's literature, arts, language, and cultural practices. His theory was that the society is attracted to the greatness of its conqueror and begins to believe that it is superior. Ibn Hazm said, "When a civilization falls, its language falls and lost, and is replaced as the conqueror takes over their land."

Arabic is a rich language capable of conveying medical sciences, making it would be far more easily and better understood by students. They would excel if they learned medicine in their mother tongue. In my lecture, I referred to a study I conducted on a group of medical students and physicians. The study revealed that students and physicians could read at a faster pace, retain more information, and comprehend better when they read the material in the Arabic. Offering medical education in the Arabic language is a necessity. However, learning one or more foreign languages and becoming fluent in them is also a must. My lecture received an overwhelmingly positive feedback and was developed into a book which was published by the Cultural Club.

This view is being shared and pushed forward by many students, physicians, and university professors across the Arab world. However, teaching Medical Sciences in Arabic is ultimately a political decision.

Several exciting experiences came my way. The late King Fahd, allotted me a piece of land in Riyadh to establish a hospital. For two years I was immersed in designing the hospital, working with hospital administrators, architects, medical planners and engineers. It was a rich new experience which I enjoyed tremendously. Needless to say, it exposed me to a world which I barely knew; the world of business. Luckily, my friend Subhi Batarji agreed to share the task of establishing the hospital with me by taking over the financial and administrative responsibility. I was finally free to go back to the world I knew and felt comfortable with: the academic world. Today, the Saudi German Hospital in Riyadh is one of the leading hospitals with 300 beds in a five-story building.

My weekly TV program "Medicine and life", which lasted 15 years enriched my life beyond words. The object of the program was to increase public awareness about disease prevention and the people's responsibility to maintain a healthy lifestyle. Perhaps, there might be another opportunity at a later date to discuss at length the goals of the program and the topics covered. However, it may be of interest to tell the story how the idea of the program was born and the series of incidents, which led to the launch of the TV program.

After I completed my postgraduate studies in tropical medicine in Germany, I returned to Saudi Arabia to work for two months as a locum in the Preventive Medicine Department at Aramco Hospital, before leaving for the United States to continue my studies in public health. That summer, I traveled with Dr. I.S. Alio, the epidemiologist in Aramco hospital, to the southern part of the country to study the problem of bilharziasis (blood-flukes). In Taif, we collected some snails (the intermediate host of the disease) from Ghadir Al Banat, a valley adjacent to Taif.

On our drive back to Taif, I stopped at the clinic of Dr. Rifaat Al-Sayed for a short visit. Dr. Rifaat was a well-known physician and the personal physician of King Faisal. He asked me to give him some snails to show to the King, who had been asking why there was bilharzia in Taif.

Days and years passed. I returned to Saudia Arabia, and was working in the Ministry of Health, when I met Dr. Rifaat again. He knew that I was still interested in infectious disease in general and bilharzia in particular. In less than a week, a telegram was sent from King Faisal to the Minister of Health requesting that I accompany a French team of physicians visiting the country to explore the problem of bilharzia. The visiting team was headed by Professor Maurice Bucaille, a gastroenterologist and an Egyptologist. In 1976, professor Bucaille published a book entitled 'The Bible, the Qur'an and Science', in which he showed that the Qur'an states marvels of astronomy, embryology, and other subjects that are in accord with modern day well established scientific findings.

During their short visit, Saudi television interviewed the team. During the interview, I had the opportunity to speak about the problem of bilharzia in the Kingdom. Shaikh Jamil Al-Hejailan, the then Minister of Information was watching the interview. A few months later, he was appointed the Minister of Health. He envisioned a television program that would educate people on important health issues and how to avoid them, and he asked if I would present it. The program 'Medicine and Life' was thus born.

During the French doctors visit, I was honored to introduce them to King Faisal. He had a majestic and imposing presence. He was tall and very eloquent., He had piercing soul searching eyes, and an awe inspiring presence. His Majesty asked how bilharzia, a disease that flourishes in freshwater snails could be so widespread – as it was then- in a dry country like Saudi Arabia. I explained to His Majesty that the snails can survive the dry periods by burying themselves in the ground. Once it rains again, the snails come out, and the life cycle resumes. Through the visitors the King made it clear that he was ready to make available all necessary resources in order to control the disease.

Every difficulty in life could be a learning experience. The mistakes we make are opportunities for learning and growth, and others can also learn and grow from our mistakes. I was fortunate enough to learn from a mistake that I made while recording the first episode of my television program, I had been searching for a guest to host for the program, and someone mentioned a prominent Arab physician who was in the Kingdom on a visit. I invited him for an interview for the program. Unfortunately, he lacked the expertise I was looking for, and to make matters worse, my tone in the interview was harsh and domineering. For fleeting moments, I felt I was in a superior position and that I had proven myself victorious over my interviewee.

Immediately after the interview, I thought over what I had just done, how I had conducted myself during the interview, and I felt ashamed of my behaviour. I forced myself to honestly rethink what had just happened. I asked myself, "Was the purpose of the television program to show off to the audience my superior knowledge over the interviewee or was it to give the public something that would add value to their lives and benefit their health?

I requested that we discard that recording and prepare a new one. I planned the method of the conduct of my interviews and prepared for my television program. I put in much effort in searching for information that would be useful and applicable to the audience; I endeavoured to present the facts, and remain objective and unbiased in my opinions. I pray that the television program did meet these goals.

Were I to ask myself today how well I delivered the message of those programs to my viewers, I would not be able to give a definite answer. No doubt, many viewers gained some health and medical information, but to what extent were they able to change their health behaviors and lifestyle? That remains the question. An added piece of information does not necessarily translate into a change in behavior. The following story illustrates my point.

I once visited one of the regions of the Kingdom to conduct a study on bilharzia. My driver took me to a flowing stream at the bottom of a valley. I collected samples of the snails attached to the rocks by the stream. I used tweezers to put the snails in a test tube, cautious not to let water touch my hand, as it could be contaminated with the bilharzia parasite. The driver offered to help. I gave him tweezers and a test tube and I showed him how to pick up the freshwater snails without touching the water. I explained to him that the snails may release into the water parasitic worms called bilharzia which cause a serious infection when contracted by humans. He worked carefully, and not even a drop of water got on his hand. However, as soon as he heard the call to prayer, he rolled his sleeves up and waded into the stream of water to perform his ablution.

Although he was given the information that the water may be polluted with parasites, he did not fully comprehend and internalize this information, and it did not affect his behavior. That is the reality of many of the public health education programs. It is easy to tell people what to do and what not to do, but one cannot guarantee that their behaviors and lifestyle habits will be influenced and changed with the newly acquired information.

The final pages of my memoirs bring me to an important point in my life, the culmination of my career. I was honored by being nominated by the

Custodian of the Two Holy Mosques to become a member of the Shoura Council, (the Consultative Assembly of Saudi Arabia). That was in the summer of the year 1993. It was a great privilege and honor, but also placed on me grave responsibilities.

This is not the time or the place to go into detail about the Shoura Council, but there are three aspects pertaining to it which I would like to mention. The first is that, all the issues brought up for deliberation were discussed with objectivity. Secondly, all Shoura Council members worked for the common good and pushed for what would bring benefits to the community, with no thought of any personal gain. Finally, the Shoura Council members developed amicable relationships. There was friendship, harmony, and respect for one another.

We learnt so much from the President of the Council, the late Sheikh Mohammed bin Jubair, may Allah have mercy upon him! He was a true role model of patience, imbued with the etiquette of discussion and discourse. We pray for the success of the current President of the Council, Sheikh Saleh bin Himaid, in carrying out the onerous responsibilities that rest upon his shoulders.

I have reached the end of my memoirs. Perhaps at a later date, I will have the opportunity to write about what the future has in store for us. The days behind us are more than those before us. I pray that Allah may guide us to the right path, keep us close to Him, and reward us for all our efforts.

Jeddah, Saudi Arabia
May 2016

Printed in the United States
By Bookmasters